HUTCHINSON ENGLISH TEXTS

Selected Poems of Pope

HUTCHINSON ENGLISH TEXTS

Selected Poems of Pope

Edited by
Philip Brockbank

HUTCHINSON EDUCATIONAL

HUTCHINSON EDUCATIONAL LTD

178–202 Great Portland Street, London, W.1

London Melbourne Sydney
Auckland Bombay Toronto
Johannesburg New York

First published November 1964
Second impression April 1967
Third impression April 1968

This book has been set in Fournier, printed in Great Britain
on Smooth Wove paper by The Anchor Press, and
bound by Wm. Brendon & Son both of Tiptree, Essex

09 072850 5

Preface

POPE is here represented by a number of complete poems, with only a token recognition of the longest pieces. There are no cuts in the poems selected, and line numbers are given for the passages in the last section.

The text is modernized in its treatment of elisions and spelling. Elisions are retained only where they would not be instinctively observed by a modern reader speaking aloud. Thus the elision is retained in *tott'ring* and *fav'rite*, and in ambiguous cases like *belov'd*, *ev'ry* and *learn'd*, but not in *warned*, *passed*, *heaven* and *even*. In most cases Pope was pushing the usage the way it was destined to go, and modern practice conforms with his intention.

Capital letters present a difficult problem and there is no solution without its crop of anomalies. Printing practice varied according to format (the larger size often having fewer capitals); the conventions within certain poems are hard to rationalize, and between different poems sometimes impossible. Nevertheless, in the manuscript and in the printed texts capitals and italics (or underlinings) are used as rhetorical scoring, and where a word seems to be deliberately stressed or solemnized it is impertinent for the editor to meddle:

> The Zeal of Fools offends at any time,
> But most of all, the Zeal of Fools in ryme.

> This calls the Church to deprecate our Sin,
> And hurls the Thunder of the Laws on *Gin*.

Capitalization has in this edition been severely reduced in *The Rape of the Lock* and in the Satire *To Mr Fortescue*, where the early editions follow the convention of capitalizing all nouns. In practice Pope's stresses fall on a very high proportion of nouns, but in his MSS and in the supervised printed texts he occasionally capitalizes adjectives and pronouns:

> Which sounds the Silver Thames along . . .
> Not but the Tragic spirit was our own . . .

Many of the poems (and all the selections) follow the Twickenham practice of retaining the typography of the first editions while admitting verbal corrections and revision from later texts.

Punctuation has not been altered except in a few cases where presentation is simplified by the use of quotation marks in place of italics for direct speech.

Page-notes are mostly explanatory, meant to economize the reader's time and leave him free to attend without annoyance to the poetry itself. Most of the notes (perhaps two-thirds) are severely abbreviated from the standard commentaries, to which I am deeply indebted: the Twickenham edition (1940–61); Elwin and Courthope (1871–89); Wakefield (1794); Warburton (1751) and the early editions supervised and annotated by Pope himself. A few notes are interpretative, directing attention to puns or other kinds of complexity; but these are meant as initiations only into the manner of the poems and make no attempt to be exhaustive or even adequate. As well as critical signposts the headnotes offer indications of the historical occasion and context of each poem, with some suggestions for further reading.

Proper names found in the text are mostly listed, with brief identities, in the Guide to Names; where a name in the page-notes carries an asterisk, more information will be found in the Guide.

The headnotes and their reading lists provide some indication of the many debts incurred to others' findings. The page-notes, however, do not attempt individual acknowledgements.

Contents

CONTENTS

Introduction

POPE'S poetry is honoured for the rare precision and intensity of its language. Through these qualities it conveys a keen sense of the possibilities of life—for good and ill—in a society which might have described itself in some of the terms used about our own: acquisitive, opulent, corrupt, enlightened, philistine, civilized and insecure. It celebrates the intricate, bountiful order of nature, and it attunes the English tongue to some of the voices of the classical past—Homer, Virgil, Ovid and Horace.

The accomplishment can be largely seen and felt for what it is through a fresh and leisured reading of the poetry itself, without fuss about literary allusiveness or about political or personal topicality. There is enough continuity in the language and literature, and in the intellectual and social life of England, for Pope to be heard still without an interpreter. And yet it is a pity to know only that aspect of the work which has in the most obvious way survived. There is more that can be revived and recovered; and historical criticism, like artificial respiration, should leave the poem breathing freely. Taken together, the headnotes to the poems that follow are meant to suggest a conspectus of Pope's development and of his growing concern with the people, ideas and events of his time. Each poem is unique, but each may be held to take its place in the larger order of the poet's vision.

It would, however, be innocent to pretend that a little sympathetic study suffices to put us wholly at ease with the art and artifice of Pope's couplets. There remains something in the modern temper which alienates us from the Augustan age. Sometimes it appears as a readiness to associate conformity with dullness, sometimes as a large distrust of artificiality. But, more particularly, we seem still reluctant to allow that manners and politics are the proper province of the poet.

It is as if D. H. Lawrence keeps us under his spell:

Poetry is, as a rule, either the voice of the far future, exquisite and ethereal, or it is the voice of the past, rich, magnificent. When the Greeks heard the *Iliad* and the *Odyssey*, they heard their own past calling in their hearts, as men far inland sometimes hear the sea and fall weak with powerful, wonderful regret, nostalgia; or else their own future rippled its time-beats through their blood, as they followed the painful, glamorous progress of the Ithacan. This was Homer to the Greeks: their Past, splendid with battles won and death achieved, and their Future, the magic wandering of Ulysses through the unknown.[1]

Pope, as translator of Homer, would have understood this (although Tennyson as author of the *Idylls of the King* and of *Ulysses* would have understood it better) but he might have felt some misgiving as Lawrence goes on:

With us it is the same. Our birds sing on the horizons. They sing out of the blue, beyond us, or out of the quenched night. They sing at dawn and sunset. Only the poor, shrill, tame canaries whistle while we talk. The wild birds begin before we are awake, or as we drop into dimness, out of waking. Our poets sit by the gateways, some by the east, some by the west. As we arrive and as we go out our hearts surge with response. But whilst we are in the midst of life, we do not hear them.

Pope by this account is a canary—very much to be heard in tne midst of life. And by Lawrence's metaphors he must be found inferior to the wild birds, or to those squatters at the gates who

1. This and the other long quotations are from 'Introduction to *New Poems*' in D. H. Lawrence, *Selected Literary Criticism*, edited by A. Beal (1955).

wait (like William Morris) for the dawn of a new life, or (like Tennyson) 'to sail beyond the sunset, and the baths of all the western stars'. But, curiously enough, Lawrence's eloquent tribute to the remoter, nostalgic kinds of poetry, accidentally recalls us to some of the qualities of Pope:

The poetry of the beginning and the poetry of the end must have that exquisite finality, perfection which belongs to all that is far off. It is in the realm of all that is perfect. It is of the nature of all that is complete and consummate. This completeness, this consummateness, the finality and perfection are conveyed in exquisite form: the perfect symmetry, the rhythm which returns upon itself like a dance where the hands link and loosen and link for the supreme moment of the end. Perfected bygone moments, perfected moments in the glimmering futurity, these are the treasured gem-like lyrics of Shelley and Keats.

It is a pity to untie Lawrence's bouquet. But is it true that only birds singing on the horizon or 'out of the quenched night' can accomplish the 'perfect symmetry' of 'exquisite form'? What of the tame canary whistling while we talk? Lawrence, unlike the Augustans[1] of England and of Rome, is reluctant to allow formal distinction to the poetry of the living present; he wants that to have other, and steeply contrasting, qualities:

But there is another kind of poetry: the poetry of that which is at hand: the immediate present. In the immediate present there is no perfection, no consummation, nothing finished. The strands are all flying, quivering, intermingling into the web, the waters are shaking the moon. There is no round, consummate moon on the face of running water, nor on the face of the unfinished tide. There are no gems of the living plasm. The living plasm vibrates unspeakably, it inhales the future, it exhales the past, it is the quick of both, and yet it is neither. There is no plasmic finality, nothing crystal, permanent. If we try to fix the

1. See below p. 159

living tissue, as the biologists fix it with formation, we have only a hardened bit of the past, the bygone life under our observation.

Magnificently said. But are there not rival claims which are equally true? Augustan civilization was fashioned from talk and Augustan man, like the Houyhnhnms of *Gulliver's Travels*, was a tamed animal. The order of society was hard won from that internecine, brutal condition that Hobbes called the state of nature; and the order of created nature was itself hard won from chaos. To stay tame required constant discipline and vigilance; the principles of orderly creation had in all senses and in all provinces to be kept up. Otherwise the 'living plasm' was likely to 'vibrate unspeakably' in quite another sense from that intended by Lawrence, with life reverting to total anarchy.

Lawrence's superb metaphor of the 'waters shaking the moon' may be met with a similar one from the Stoic philosopher Epictetus. By this, the tumults of the outside world are reflected in the water of the mind, and when the mind is composed all the images held in its stillness are of a true and therefore acceptable shape. It is so too with the finely 'composed' poetry of Pope; the polished surface holds its images of life without distortion.

For Lawrence the remoteness of perfection from the immediate present yields two distinctly different kinds of poetry—one nostalgic and of 'exquisite form', and the other with 'come-and-go, not-fixity, inconclusiveness, immediacy, the quality of life itself, without dénouement or close'. In the work of Pope form and quickness are wedded, though tensions between them remain.

We can find a concern for perfection, for the idyllic past and for exquisite form in the Discourse and poems of Pope's earliest published work, the *Pastorals* of 1709. 'The pastoral', he tells us, 'is an image of what they call the Golden Age.' In it, the prose and the poetry assure us, life was ordered by a pure, ritual simplicity of dance and song. Even if the symmetries of pastoral mock the confusions of the present, they can be recovered by the poet's art and so appease the tantalizing human itch for tranquillity.

Although in his Pastorals Pope is singing 'on the horizons', we may detect in them an eagerness to call the idyll back from ancient Greece and Rome to modern England:

> O'er golden sands let rich Pactolus flow,
> And trees weep amber on the banks of Po!
> Blest Thames's shores the brightest beauties yield,
> Feed here my lambs, I'll seek no distant field.

Pope was to bring the pastoral dream nearer to the heart of contemporary life. He wrote the *Messiah*, a 'sacred Eclogue' composed of passages from Isaiah and 'written in imitation of Virgil's Pollio'. Steele published it in *The Spectator* (14 May 1712) as the work of a friend 'who is not ashamed to employ his wit in the praise of his Maker'. But the poem which would have been more obviously of interest to readers of *The Spectator* is *Windsor Forest* (1713). It is not technically a pastoral because not a sustained imitation of either Theocritus or Virgil but, while the manner is strictly contemporary, Pope is still echoing the messianic tones of Isaiah and the Pollio:

> The groves of *Eden*, vanished now so long,
> Live in description, and look green in song:
> *These*, were my breast inspired with equal flame,
> Like them in beauty, should be like in fame.
> Here hills and vales, the woodland and the plain,
> Here earth and water seem to strive again;
> Not *chaos*-like together crushed and bruised,
> But, as the world harmoniously confused:
> Where Order in Variety we see,
> And where, though all things differ, all agree.

The grounds of Windsor recall the groves of Eden, and the poet's song must imitate the symmetry and rich variety of both—it too is 'harmoniously confused' and brings differing things into agreement.

13

The poem goes on to show that those confusions of the world that are not harmonious are the responsibility of man throughout his history, and the outrages committed upon the brightness and innocence of the pastoral order are particularly the work of man the hunter. The hunter comes from the pastoral world and he destroys it. But hunting is at the same time symbolic of all the natural energies that by metamorphosis might recover the golden age; swords, as in *Isaiah* and in Pope's *Messiah*, might be beaten into ploughshares. The poem recalls the England of Queen Anne to its paradisal inheritance:

> Here Ceres' gifts in waving prospect stand,
> And nodding tempt the joyful reaper's hand;
> Rich Industry sits smiling on the plains,
> And peace and plenty tell, a STUART reigns.

And it concludes with a vision of mercantile prosperity, secured by the Peace of Utrecht, with London at the heart of an exotic, vastly prolific and various empire, safe from violence and sustained by freedom.

What is 'exquisite and etherial' belongs for Pope, not to some glimmering unsatisfied desire, but to a specific condition of life and to a specific poetic form. *Windsor Forest* genuinely nourishes what Addison found in Sir Andrew Freeport—the more noble and generous notions of trade.

Pope was to grow more sceptical as he lived on through Walpole's regime. But he never ceased to be interested in the quality of leisured life in the country house, and its relationship to a richly human civilization sustained by agriculture and commerce. The *Epistle to Burlington* returns, with maturer art and insight, to the themes of *Windsor Forest*.

In the latest poetry, written when Pope's friends were mostly to be found among the Patriots (the disappointed and disenchanted opposition party), the pastoral dream has almost totally faded. But the garden remains, and the motif of retreat keeps a moving and refreshing power:

Oft, in the clear, still mirror of retreat,
I studied Shrewsbury, the wise and great.

Pope, in his own Twickenham garden or in the gardens of
Bathurst or Cobham, looked upon Westminster and the City as
Horace had looked upon Rome from the serene distance of his
country villa. But again retreat is not escape. The calm mind, like
the still garden lake, is a clearer mirror and offers a clearer image
of reality.

Quite as important as the pastoral theme itself are the skills
that Pope taught himself in the course of writing and re-writing
his pastoral poetry. He found out how to evoke idyllic serenity
by chimes of the tongue with the sense, echoing cadences, symmetrical figures and a hard limpidity of diction.[1] Once the ear is
tuned to the manner, the imagination finds itself caught in haunt-
ing reminiscences of a world of classic simplicity and delicacy.
Every little catastrophe occurring within it is an outrage both
upon nature and upon art. The pheasant shot in *Windsor Forest* is
not only natural but also marvellously artificial, not only alive but
also exquisitely designed—it has 'scarlet-circled eyes', 'painted
wings' and a 'breast that flames with gold'. But the artifice is not
hostile to life. On the contrary, artifice cherishes life. The poet
feels that his 're-creation' must imitate the skill and precision of
Creation itself—an antique idea of the divine role of the poet that
drives through Pope's poetry to *The Dunciad*.

The Rape of the Lock harvests much from the early pastoral.
The same art now discovers all that is proudly feminine, etherial
and captivating in the manners of high society:

Smooth flow the waves, the zephyrs gently play,
Belinda smiled, and all the world was gay.

But the idyll despoiled in *Windsor Forest* is simpler and more
innocent by far than the fragile, finely sophisticated honour of

1. See pages 195, 196

Belinda. Sophisticated ladies, as we shall be reminded in the *Epistle to a Lady*, delighted in posing as nymphs of Arcady. Pastoral innocence had itself become a modish vanity, and Pope was sensitive to the irony.

Pope's irony, however, has many other sources too. *The Rape of the Lock* as often recalls us to his skill in epic as in pastoral poetry. Along with the Pastorals he had published an episode from *The Iliad*, and in 1712 a rendering of Statius (*Thebais* I) which he said he had written in his childhood. The splendour of battles long ago and the glamour of strange wanderings had cast their enchantment on the boy and on the ambitious poet. At intervals between 1715 and 1726 he brought out his full version of Homer. For all its energy, buoyancy and dignity it is, to revert to Lawrence's metaphor, a tamed Homer—better fitted for recital in a drawing-room than at a popular public festival.

As Dr Johnson was to reflect, even Virgil, who was so much nearer to Homer in language and date, found 'the state of the world so much altered, and the demand for elegance so much increased, that mere nature could be endured no longer'. 'One refinement', he says, 'makes for another, and what was expedient to Virgil was necessary to Pope.' Homer had to be mediated to the taste of the age, a taste that Johnson himself found over-sophisticated: 'a saturated intellect soon becomes luxurious, and knowledge finds no willing reception till it is recommended by artificial diction'. But it is also proper to remember that 'mere nature' had not the same aspect in Homer's Greece as it had in Virgil's Rome and Pope's London. Each civilization required from its representative figures a different kind of human excellence, and therefore from its poets a different kind of propriety of language. What is at work in much of the language of Pope's Homer is an eagerness to lessen the distance between the antique hero and the eighteenth-century gentleman; and this could be accomplished (as Dryden too had understood) by resolving the Olympian dialect of Milton into the polite fluency of Waller.

Pope was well aware of the remoteness of his world from the

militant, heroic communities of antiquity. He takes occasion from Horace's wry reflections on the prevalence of Greek civilization over Roman military strength to make the same point about France and England:

> We conquered France, but felt our captive's charms;
> Her arts victorious triumphed o'er our arms:
> Britain to soft refinements less a foe,
> Wit grew polite, and numbers learned to flow.
> (*To Augustus* 263–6)

Here, as in *The Rape of the Lock*, we find an archness that both mocks and indulges the 'soft refinements'; 'our captive's charms' is in the manner of Restoration-stage lyric—France has become England's mistress.

But the France that wins Pope's recognition has its austere quality too:

> Late, very late, correctness grew our care,
> When the tired nation breathed from civil war.
> Exact Racine and Corneille's noble fire
> Showed us that France had something to admire.

Not all modes of refinement are soft. Some are authentically heroic. Take, for example, Pope's highly wrought rendering of the death of Villiers, second Duke of Buckingham, in many ways a Restoration hero:

> In the worst inn's worst room, with mat half-hung,
> The floors of plaister, and the walls of dung,
> On once a flock-bed, but repaired with straw,
> With tape-tied curtains never meant to draw,
> The George and Garter dangling from that bed
> Where tawdry yellow strove with dirty red,
> Great Villiers lies,—alas! how changed from him,
> That life of pleasure, and that soul of whim!

> Gallant and gay, in Cliveden's proud alcove,
> The bower of wanton Shrewsbury and love;
> Or just as gay, at Council, in a ring
> Of mimicked statesmen, and their merry King.
> No Wit to flatter left of all his store!
> No Fool to laugh at, which he valued more.
> There, Victor of his health, of fortune, friends,
> And fame; this lord of useless thousands ends.

The fall of Villiers is the fall of a great house and of the civilization that graced it. The walls of the inn (it is no longer a home) are cheaply fashioned from wattle and daub, the floor from a gypsum cement; splendour reverts to dirt and dust. Pope is distantly recalling the death of Hector and the fall of Troy:

> The thronging Greeks behold with wond'ring eyes
> His manly beauty and superior size:
> While some, ignobler, the great dead deface
> With wounds ungen'rous or with taunts disgrace.
> 'How changed that Hector! who like Jove of late
> Sent lightning on our fleets, and scattered fate.'
>
> .   .   .   .   .
>
> Is not Troy fall'n already? Haste, ye powers!
> See, if already their deserted towers
> Are left unmanned; or if they yet retain
> The souls of heroes, their great Hector slain.

But what is recalled is not imitated. The excellence of Villiers was of another kind than Hector's. It is an excellence that allows all the stress to fall on courtesy, gaiety and elegance in 'gallant', and admits the suggestion that Villiers owed his power to his skill in mockery.

Mockery had indeed an extraordinary potency in the Augustan period, with the self-consciously decorous élites of both parties valuing it as a means of securing conformity among equals. The

Earl of Shaftesbury offered a systematic account of it in his highly readable and revealing *Essay on the Freedom of Wit and Humour* (1709). His idea of freedom is precisely and disarmingly restricted: 'I write in defence only of the liberty of the Club, and of that sort of freedom which is taken among gentlemen and friends who know one another perfectly well.' 'All politeness is owing to liberty', he tells us, and 'we polish one another and rub off our corners and rough sides by a sort of amicable collision.' In his *Letter Concerning Enthusiasm* he claims that 'Never was there in our nation a time when folly and extravagance of every kind were more sharply inspected or more wittily ridiculed'. And the serious can be distinguished from the ridiculous only 'by applying ridicule to see if it will bear'.

Pope's role was clear in the kind of society that Shaftesbury describes. In pastoral he could refresh its imagery of the golden age, in epic translation recall the nobility of the heroic age and in a poetry of mockery keep folly and fanaticism from breaking into the citadels of the Augustan age. He could perform, too, the kind of service that Shaftesbury himself undertook, by setting down in the lucid and urbane aphorisms of the *Essay on Criticism* and the *Essay on Man* the assumptions (stable and unstable) on which polite literature and life flourished in the early eighteenth century.

In his poetry of mockery Pope owes a deep, and fully acknowledged, debt to Horace. It is from Horace and from the earlier English Horatians (Jonson, for example, and Marvell) that Pope acquired some of his poise—touching on the one hand the lyrical and heroic potentials of the language, and on the other its potentials for analysis and indictment—often compelling from us at the same moment the judgements 'how beautiful' and 'how severe!' Pope's Horatian 'song' modulates at will into colloquial speech. It reaches actual talk in much the same way as in its matter it seems to reach actual cases, not mere fictions. It is brought home, into 'the midst of life', into a familiar state of society.

But it does not therefore follow that it bids farewell to 'form'. Like Lawrence the Augustans were sensitive to the hostilities that make themselves felt between Form and Life; one of the jokes of Swift's Laputa is that organic life and mathematical and musical form are irreconcilable—beef there is absurdly cut into rhomboids, ducks trussed up as fiddles and pudding made into a cycloid. But they nevertheless believed that 'form' could in some senses contain and intensify life without damage to the living tissue. Hogarth in his *Analysis of Beauty* finds that some corset-stays have an aptly natural form while others have a bad mechanical one.

Lawrence, in his anxiety to repudiate mechanical form, was apt to undervalue all modes of conformity. Writing of Thomas Mann, but glancing in passing at what he calls the 'logical expressions of the school of Pope', he asks: 'Can the human mind fix absolutely the definite line of a book, any more than it can fix absolutely any definite line of action for a human being?' No, it can't. But 'absolutely' is a formidable word, and it must not daunt us into forgetting that life will yield to order if we discover and impose the right kind.

When Lawrence says that 'the living plasm vibrates unspeakably', no Augustan could take pleasure in that disturbing word 'unspeakably'; let it rather vibrate 'speakably' in coherent, articulate order. Pope knew that spawning and breeding life can get out of hand and creation confound itself. If the order of nature is to flourish it must be cultivated, as Shakespeare reminds us when he has Hamlet say of the world:

> Fie on't, ah fie, 'tis an unweeded garden
> That grows to seed, things rank and gross in nature
> Possess it merely.

What applies to the natural applies to the moral world since moral deformities are also perversions of growth.

Pope's attack on the poetaster 'Codrus' can serve to show how energy and form can be perverted. The bad playwright, as Pope reveals him, is a bad creator and upsets the miraculous design of the world by behaving without proper regard to his place in it. To write plays with thin plots and flimsy dialogue is to behave, as Pope's wit has it, like a spider:

> Throned in the centre of his thin designs
> Proud of a vast extent of flimsy lines.
> *(To Arbuthnot* 93–4)

It is beautifully said about the spider, but severely said about the man. The energies of life must be properly directed, and a man must not be like a spider or, to take examples from elsewhere in the poetry, like a beetle, or a rooting hog, or a blow-fly. Man must be true to his place in the chain of being; but Codrus doubly offends—his pride is like a God's and his performance like an insect's. Hence he deserves the sharp colloquial dismissal which puts him in his place:

> The creature's at his dirty work again.

All the men or 'creatures' exposed to Pope's purging wrath or to his bantering insinuations are so because of a failure to honour an exacting code of behaviour and certain precise expectations about human nature. This is not to say that Pope always fairly represents his victims in his verse; only that the criteria of judgement are consistent and stringent.

The organization and cultivation which are the proper inheritance of man if he exercises his understanding and good sense, carry with them a range of responsibilities which we are free to call 'Augustan'. Creation is a social system and we cannot afford to see it as anything else:

> Look round our world; behold the chain of love
> Combining all below and all above.

> See plastic Nature working to this end,
> The single atoms each to other tend,
> Attract, attracted to, the next in place
> Formed and impelled its neighbour to embrace.
>
> (*Essay on Man* III 7 ff.)

The social order, like the dance that Pope insinuates into his couplets, is a system of mutual exchanges, an orderly linking of hands.

The tradition that Pope salutes in his exemplary aphorism, 'The proper study of mankind is man', is older than Aristotle and will, one hopes, stretch to the crack of doom—however imminent or remote that might be. It is not hard to reconcile with Christianity. And yet the *Essay on Man*, felicitously acclaiming the goodness and wisdom of Providence, and endorsing the sanctity of the golden mean, seems to declare an innocent faith in human perfectibility. Pope warns us about the instabilities of the system:

> Let earth, unbalanced, from her orbit fly,
> Planets and suns run lawless through the sky;
> Let ruling angels from their spheres be hurled,
> Being on being wrecked, and world on world;
> Heaven's whole foundations to their centre nod,
> And Nature trembles to the throne of God.
> All this dread order break—for whom? for thee?
> Vile worm!—oh madness! pride! impiety!

But we find the warnings less memorable than the reassurances:

> All Nature is but art, unknown to thee
> All chance, direction, which thou canst not see;
> All discord, harmony not understood;
> All partial evil, universal good:
> And, spite of pride, in erring reason's spite,
> One truth is clear, Whatever is, is Right.

As Pope moved on to perfect his design, however, and turned from his large, Olympian survey of man to his critical inspection of the 'vile worms', the reassurances are muted.

In the Horatian poems increasingly, in the last book of *The Dunciad* and in the two-part *Epilogue to the Satires*, the crack of doom seems imminent indeed. The whole structure—from God to gosling—begins to lurch. Nevertheless, the order of the poet's art still has its resources; the imagery of chaos is controlled in an exhilarating verse; and we can enjoy the last poems as we enjoy certain Old Testament prophets, with the proud sense of keeping our bearings in a void.

It might be argued, however, from ample evidence, that the pessimistic mood of the late poetry was owed to the frustration of the political party (the Tory Patriots) to which Pope kept his loyalty. Commercial interests, represented in *The Dunciad* by Smithfield and the City, seemed to him increasingly to dominate the culture of his society, while the great house and the paternal landed aristocracy played a diminishing and more provincial part. But what Pope feared was the eclipse not of a particular political interest but of the cultivated and humane way of life which that interest at its best represented, and which in all its supple variety is plainly exhibited to us in the Horatian poems.

There are, of course, flaws and defects in Pope's allegiances and in the causes to which they were owed. The time comes when it is necessary to challenge the whole structure of Augustan thought and feeling and to cry with Blake: 'Damn braces: Bless relaxes.' But challenges are vain and silly if they are made without acknowledgement and intimate understanding of the fine and vigorous validity of the whole vision.

SOME TESTS OF ART

Although an exacting form the heroic couplet is not a monotonous one. It has an immense range of expressive effects, from the most remote and sonorous to the easy, conversational and fragmentary. Little is gained by attempting for each line a conventional kind of scansion, but it is nevertheless an advantage to hear how the live reading rides with or against the formal basic metre. Here it rides with:

> So round and round the ghosts of beauty glide

and here, against:

> Then, like the sun, let bounty spread her ray
> And shine that superfluity away

The syntax offers another kind of movement that might also ride with or against the basic metre:

> Flights of Cashiers, or Mobs, he'll never mind;
> And knows no losses while the Muse is kind.
> To cheat a Friend, or Ward, he leaves to Peter;
> The good man heaps up nothing but mere metre,
> Enjoys his Garden and his Book in quiet;
> And then—a perfect Hermit in his Diet.

Pope's own technical prescriptions in *An Essay on Criticism* deserve close study (an extract is given on p. 198) and so do Johnson's comments in his *Life of Pope*. There is some good close analysis of the couplet in Donald Davie's *Articulate Energy* and in Wilson Knight's *The Burning Oracle*.

Some hints for the reading of particular couplets are offered in the notes and introductions, but there is little that cannot be reached by vigilant reading and by full use of the *Oxford English Dictionary*.

Ode on Solitude

An EARLY poem, modelled largely on Horace's second epode.
It is first found in the letter to Cromwell of 17 July 1709, and
was first printed in 1717. To see how the calm movement of the
poem is attained, compare these early versions of stanza 1:

How happy he, who free from care,
  The rage of courts, and noise of towns;
Contented breath[e]s his native air,
            In his own grounds.   (1717)

Happy the Man, who free from Care,
  The Business and the Noise of Towns,
Contented breath[e]s his Native Air,
            In his own Grounds.   (MS 1727)

In 1717 'soft' in line 10 was 'swift'. The 1727 MS version of the
line is 'His years slide silently away'. The typography follows the
1717 edition.

ODE ON SOLITUDE

Happy the man, whose wish and care
  A few paternal acres bound,
Content to breathe his native air,
            In his own ground.

Whose herds with milk, whose fields with bread,
    Whose flocks supply him with attire,
Whose trees in summer yield him shade,
                In winter fire.

Blest! who can unconcern'dly find
    Hours, days, and years slide soft away,
In health of body, peace of mind,
                Quiet by day,

Sound sleep by night; study and ease,
    Together mixed; sweet recreation:
And innocence, which most does please,
                With meditation.

Thus let me live, unseen, unknown;
    Thus unlamented let me die;
Steal from the world, and not a stone
                Tell where I lie.

The Rape of the Lock

THIS poem was first written with the diplomatic purpose of reconciling, at the request of Pope's friend John Caryll, the quarrel occasioned between Lady Arabella Fermor and Caryll's relative Lord Petre by an actual 'rape' of a lock in the summer of 1711. It was quickly written and from the first met with better literary than diplomatic success. Sir George Brown (the Sir Plume of the piece) took offence; and it is possible that Lady Arabella was herself dismayed at the publicity that she received through the 1712 edition, when hostile critics noticed the hysteria and the bawdry attributed to Belinda and hinted that the satire was at her expense.

The 1712 poem was in two parts and only 334 lines long. Pope added the 'machinery' (see the dedication) together with the game of ombre and the cave of spleen in 1713, making the present five cantos. Clarissa's speech in Canto V was added in 1717 (see note v 9).

In a manner both light and commanding, Pope presents a sophisticated social catastrophe as at once momentous and trivial. It is momentous because the exquisite feminine graces of Belinda testify to the sanctity of the 'cosmetic powers' and a Lady's chastity (like the frail China jar associated with it in the poem's dainty symbolism) is easily flawed. It is trivial because so remote from the world of heroic action for which, as the verse by its accomplishment assures us, the poet has expectantly tuned his lyre.

Most of the effects can be caught by alert reading of the poem itself, but the allusiveness enriches what we might call its orchestration. When, for example, Pope writes:

> Her joy in gilded chariots when alive,
> And love of *ombre*, after death survive.

he reminds us in a note of *Aeneid* vi 653, which Dryden rendered:

> The love of horses which they had, alive,
> And care of chariots, after death survive.   (vi 890)

'Chariot' was a word still used for coaches.

Similarly, the epic apostrophe in Canto III (101 ff.) echoes Dryden's *Aeneid* x 698:

> O Mortals! blind in fate, who never know
> To bear high fortune, or endure the low!
> The time shall come, when Turnus, but in vain,
> Shall wish untouched the trophies of the slain—
> Shall wish the fatal belt were far away,
> And curse the dire remembrance of the day.

Other mock-epics (Vida's *Game of Chess*, for example, and Boileau's *Le Lutrin*) had already helped to establish a convention that Pope was free to embellish and perfect.

Not only the heroic but also the pastoral modes are recalled by allusion and imitation, and the closing lines sustain the poem's irony with a beautifully authentic pathos. It is very much an eighteenth-century art that permits this felicitous suspension of sincerity in pretence. Mozart's *Così fan Tutte* is clearly of the same civilization, and so for different reasons is the art of Hogarth and Rowlandson. In Hogarth's *Rake's Progress* (Soane Museum) the mistress's levée is rendered with some of the affection and sharpness that Pope brings to Belinda's toilet; the plate 'Noon' in the *Times of the Day* series has a beau of the 'Sir Plume' kind: while for some impression of the poise of aristocratic manners at their best there is Hogarth's 'Strode Family' in the National Gallery. Rowlandson's water-colours, beautifully subtle and translucent in texture but virulent in judgement, offer something like a visual equivalent of Pope's delicate and severe art.

The notes here owe much to Geoffrey Tillotson's Twickenham volume, which has a valuable history and critical estimate of the poem. An excellent survey and analysis is offered by J. S. Cunningham, *Pope: The Rape of the Lock* (1961), which has a useful reading-list for further study. Reuben Brower, *Alexander Pope: The Poetry of Allusion* (1959) is essential for a full understanding of the poem's literary sophistication.

It is an interesting exercise to compare the first version (printed in the Twickenham edition pp. 127–37) with the second. It will be noticed that the second version is made to open out of Belinda's deliciously drowsy morning dream, and it is in this that the vision of the 'thousand bright inhabitants of air' is first entertained. Here are lines 7–20 of the 1712 edition:

Say what strange Motive, Goddess! cou'd compel
A well-bred *Lord* t'assault a gentle *Belle*?
Oh say what stranger Cause, yet unexplor'd,
Cou'd make a gentle *Belle* reject a *Lord*?
And dwells such Rage in *softest Bosoms* then?
And lodge such daring Souls in *Little Men*?
Sol thro' white Curtains did his Beams display
And op'd those Eyes which brighter shine than they;
Shock just had giv'n himself the rowzing Shake,
And Nymphs prepar'd their *Chocolate* to take;
Thrice the wrought Slipper knock'd against the Ground,
And striking Watches the tenth Hour resound.
Belinda rose, and 'midst attending Dames
Launch'd on the Bosom of the silver *Thames*.

In the present edition the capitals of the 1714 text have been much reduced, but the italics have been generally retained.

THE RAPE OF THE LOCK

DEDICATION TO MRS ARABELLA FERMOR

MADAM, It will be in vain to deny that I have some regard for this piece, since I dedicate it to you. Yet you may bear me witness, it was intended only to divert a few young ladies, who have good sense and good humour enough, to laugh not only at their sex's little unguarded follies, but at their own. But as it was communicated with the air of a secret, it soon found its way into the world. An imperfect copy having been offered to a bookseller, you had the good-nature for my sake to consent to the publication of one more correct: this I was forced to before I had executed half my design, for the *machinery* was entirely wanting to complete it.

The *machinery*, Madam, is a term invented by the critics, to signify that part which the Deities, Angels, or Dæmons are made to act in a Poem: for the ancient Poets are in one respect like many modern ladies; let an action be never so trivial in itself, they always make it appear of the utmost importance. These machines I determined to raise on a very new and odd foundation, the *Rosicrucian* doctrine of Spirits.

I know how disagreeable it is to make use of hard words before a lady; but 'tis so much the concern of a Poet to have his works understood, and particularly by your sex, that you must give me leave to explain two or three difficult terms.

The *Rosicrucians* are a people I must bring you acquainted with. The best account I know of them is in a French book called *Le Comte de Gabalis*, which both in its title and size is so like a novel that many of the fair sex have read it for one by mistake. According to these gentlemen, the four elements are inhabited by Spirits which they call *Sylphs, Gnomes, Nymphs* and *Salamanders*. The *Gnomes*, or Dæmons of Earth, delight in mischief; but the

Sylphs, whose habitation is in the air, are the best-conditioned creatures imaginable. For they say, any mortals may enjoy the most intimate familiarities with these gentle Spirits, upon a condition very easy to all true *Adepts*, an inviolate preservation of chastity.

As to the following Cantos, all the passages of them are as fabulous as the vision at the beginning, or the transformation at the end; (except the loss of your hair, which I always mention with reverence). The human persons are as fictitious as the airy ones; and the character of Belinda, as it is now managed, resembles you in nothing but in beauty.

If this Poem had as many graces as there are in your person, or in your mind, yet I could never hope it should pass through the world half so uncensured as you have done. But let its fortune be what it will, mine is happy enough, to have given me this occasion of assuring you that I am, with the truest esteem, *Madam, Your Most Obedient Humble Servant,*

A. POPE.

"I was reluctant, Belinda, to cut off your look but I am happy to have granted this to your wishes."

Nolueram, Belinda, tuos violare capillos,
Sed juvat hoc precibus me tribuisse tuis.—MARTIAL XII 84

absurdity of convention of the structure & formality of society Caryling against the

CANTO I

WHAT dire offence from am'rous causes springs,
What mighty contests rise from trivial things,
I sing—This verse to *Caryll*, Muse! is due;
This, ev'n *Belinda* may vouchsafe to view:
Slight is the subject, but not so the praise,   5
If she inspire, and he approve my lays.

3 *I sing* the verb usually concludes the epic 'proposition'; see the opening of *Paradise Lost*. 5–6 follow *Georgic* iv 6 in Dryden's and Sedley's translations

Say what strange motive, Goddess! could compel
A well-bred *Lord* t' assault a gentle *Belle*?
O say what stranger cause, yet unexplored,
Could make a gentle *Belle* reject a *Lord*?   10
In tasks so bold, can little men engage,
And in soft bosoms dwells such mighty rage?
  Sol through white curtains shot a timorous ray,
And oped those eyes that must eclipse the day:
Now lapdogs give themselves the rowzing shake,   15
And sleepless lovers, just at twelve awake:
Thrice rung the bell, the slipper knocked the ground,
And the pressed watch returned a silver sound.
Belinda still her downy pillow pressed,
Her guardian *Sylph* prolonged the balmy rest.   20
'Twas he had summoned to her silent bed
The morning-dream that hovered o'er her head.
A youth more glitt'ring than a *Birth-night Beau*,
(That ev'n in slumber caused her cheek to glow)
Seemed to her ear his winning lips to lay,   25
And thus in whispers said, or seemed to say:
  'Fairest of mortals, thou distinguished care
Of thousand bright inhabitants of air!
If e'er one vision touched thy infant thought,
Of all the nurse and all the priest have taught,   30
Of airy elves by moonlight shadows seen,
The silver token, and the circled green,
Or Virgins visited by Angel-Powers,
With golden crowns and wreaths of heavenly flowers;
Hear and believe! thy own importance know,   35
Nor bound thy narrow views to things below.

11 little men i.e. all mankind; but particularly short men like Lord Petre *12*
Dryden's *Aeneid* I 11: 'Can heavenly minds such high resentment show?' *17 bell*
a hand-bell *18 pressed watch* a 'repeater' which sounded the hour when its pin
was pressed *23 birth-night* royal birthday ball *32 silver token* left by the fairies in
the slippers of good house-maids *circled* i.e. with fairy-rings *33 Virgins visited* the
Annunciation; and similar experiences of the saints

Some secret truths, from learned pride concealed,
To maids alone and children are revealed:
What, though no credit doubting wits may give?
The fair and innocent shall still believe.   40
Know then, unnumbered spirits round thee fly,
The light *militia* of the lower sky;
These, though unseen, are ever on the wing,
Hang o'er the *box*, and hover round the *Ring*.
Think what an equipage thou hast in air,   45
And view with scorn *two pages* and a *chair*.
As now your own, our beings were of old,
And once inclosed in woman's beauteous mould;
Thence, by a soft transition, we repair
From earthly vehicles to these of air.   50
Think not, when woman's transient breath is fled,
That all her vanities at once are dead:
Succeeding vanities she still regards,
And though she plays no more, o'erlooks the cards.
Her joy in gilded chariots, when alive,   55
And love of *ombre*, after death survive.
For when the fair in all their pride expire,
To their first elements their souls retire:
The sprites of fiery termagants in flame
Mount up, and take a Salamander's name.   60
Soft yielding minds to water glide away,
And sip, with *Nymphs*, their elemental tea.
The graver prude sinks downward to a *Gnome*,
In search of mischief still on earth to roam.

37–8 see Matthew xi 25 *42 lower sky* i.e. of air, not aether *44 box* theatre-box *Ring* see p. 94 *45 equipage* carriage with horses and footmen *46 chair* sedan *50 vehicles* materials in which spiritual forms can take shape; with pun on equipage and chair *55 chariots* then a common term for coaches; see headnote *56 ombre* the card-game *58 first elements* i.e. whichever is primary in their nature *59 fiery termagant* hot-tempered shrew, whose dominant element is fire *60 Salamander* creature fabled to live in fire *62 elemental tea* because brewed from water, the Nymphs' element

The light coquettes in *Sylphs* aloft repair,   65
And sport and flutter in the fields of air.
    'Know farther yet; whoever fair and chaste
Rejects mankind, is by some *Sylph* embraced:
For spirits, freed from mortal laws, with ease
Assume what sexes and what shapes they please.   70
What guards the purity of melting maids,
In courtly balls, and midnight masquerades,
Safe from the treach'rous friend, the daring spark,
The glance by day, the whisper in the dark;
When kind occasion prompts their warm desires,   75
When music softens, and when dancing fires?
'Tis but their *Sylph*, the wise celestials know,
Though *Honour* is the word with men below.
    'Some Nymphs there are, too conscious of their face,
For life predestined to the *Gnome's* embrace.   80
These swell their prospects and exalt their pride,
When offers are disdained, and love denied.
Then gay ideas crowd the vacant brain;
While peers and dukes, and all their sweeping train,
And garters, stars, and coronets appear,   85
And in soft sounds, 'Your Grace' salutes their ear.
'Tis these that early taint the female soul,
Instruct the eyes of young *Coquettes* to roll,
Teach infant cheeks a bidden blush to know,
And little hearts to flutter at a *Beau*.   90
    'Oft when the world imagine women stray,
The *Sylphs* through mystic mazes guide their way,
Through all the giddy circle they pursue,
And old impertinence expel by new.

69–70 follow *Paradise Lost* I 423–32 *spark* dandy *88 Spectator* 46 has an
'Ogling-master' *89 bidden blush* is this the cosmetic blush of line **143**? *92 mystic*
mysterious, esoteric *93 giddy circle* i.e. social round *94 impertinence* trifling
folly

What tender maid but must a victim fall   95
To one man's treat, but for another's ball?
When *Florio* speaks, what virgin could withstand,
If gentle *Damon* did not squeeze her hand?
With varying vanities, from ev'ry part,
They shift the moving toy-shop of their heart;   100
Where wigs with wigs, with sword-knots sword-knots strive,
Beaus banish beaus, and coaches coaches drive.
This erring mortals levity may call,
Oh, blind to truth! the *Sylphs* contrive it all.

'Of these am I, who thy protection claim,   105
A watchful sprite, and *Ariel* is my name.
Late, as I ranged the crystal wilds of air,
In the clear mirror of thy ruling *Star*
I saw, alas! some dread event impend,
Ere to the main this morning sun descend.   110
But heaven reveals not what, or how, or where:
Warned by thy *Sylph*, oh pious maid beware!
This to disclose is all thy guardian can:
Beware of all, but most beware of man!'
He said; when *Shock*, who thought she slept too long,   115
Leapt up, and waked his mistress with his tongue.
'Twas then *Belinda!* if report say true,
Thy eyes first opened on a *Billet-doux;*
Wounds, charms, and *ardours,* were no sooner read,
But all the vision vanished from thy head.   120
And now, unveiled, the *Toilet* stands displayed,
Each silver vase in mystic order laid.

96 treat 'an entertainment of food and drink' (O.E.D.) *97 Florio* name suggesting
'flower of youth' *98 Damon* conventional name for pastoral swain *101 sword-
knots* ribbons tied to hilt; often a mistress's favour *102 drive* an infelicitous pun?
105 thy protection i.e. 'I claim to protect thee' *107–14* compare *Paradise Lost*
iv 561–88 *108 clear mirror* 'the language of the Platonists' (Pope): combined
with the astrological notion that stars show the truth *115 Shock* or 'shough', a
kind of poodle *117–18* i.e. if report say true this is her first love letter *122 mystic
order* i.e. like the furniture of an altar

First, robed in white, the nymph intent adores
With head uncovered, the *Cosmetic* Powers.
A heavenly image in the glass appears,   125
To that she bends, to that her eye she rears;
Th' inferior priestess, at her altar's side,
Trembling, begins the sacred Rites of Pride.
Unnumbered treasures ope at once, and here
The various off'rings of the world appear;   130
From each she nicely culls with curious toil,
And decks the Goddess with the glitt'ring spoil.
This casket *India's* glowing gems unlocks,
And all *Arabia* breathes from yonder box.
The tortoise here and elephant unite,   135
Transformed to combs, the speckled and the white.
Here files of pins extend their shining rows,
Puffs, powders, patches, bibles, billet-doux.
Now awful beauty puts on all its arms;
The fair each moment rises in her charms,   140
Repairs her smiles, awakens every grace,
And calls forth all the wonders of her face:
Sees by degrees a purer blush arise,
And keener lightnings quicken in her eyes.
The busy *Sylphs* surround their darling care;   145
These set the head, and those divide the hair,
Some fold the sleeve, while others plait the gown;
And *Betty's* praised for labours not her own.

---

123 robed in white dressing gown, suggesting vestal garment *132 the Goddess* i.e. the image in her glass *135–6* a mock Ovidian metamorphosis? *138* Charles Montagu had written, 'Prayer-book, patch-boxes, sermon-notes and paint'. *patches* beauty-patches *bibles* the plural suggests the dainty rather than the useful kind *144 keener lightnings* belladonna (deadly nightshade) was sometimes used to make eyes sparkle

CANTO II

Not with more glories, in th' etherial plain,
The sun first rises o'er the purpled main,
Than issuing forth, the rival of his beams
Launched on the bosom of the silver *Thames*.
Fair nymphs and well-dressed youths around her shone, 5
But ev'ry eye was fixed on her alone. *the extent her honour*
On her white breast a sparkling *Cross* she wore, *allows*
Which *Jews* might kiss, and infidels adore.
Her lively looks a sprightly mind disclose,
Quick as her eyes, and as unfixed as those: 10
Favours to none, to all she smiles extends;
Oft she rejects, but never once offends.
Bright as the sun, her eyes the gazers strike,
And, like the sun, they shine on all alike.
Yet graceful ease, and sweetness void of pride, 15
Might hide her faults, if *Belles* had faults to hide:
If to her share some female errors fall, *Pope acknowledges beau-*
Look on her face, and you'll forget 'em all. *ty its power despite the*
 This nymph, to the destruction of mankind, *irrationalities of*
Nourished two locks, which graceful hung behind 20 *the female mind*
In equal curls, and well conspired to deck
With shining ringlets the smooth iv'ry neck.
Love in these labyrinths his slaves detains,
And mighty hearts are held in slender chains.
With hairy springes we the birds betray, 25
Slight lines of hair surprise the finny prey,

4 launched on set out upon; river craft went between London and Hampton Court
14 see Matthew v 45 *25 springes* snares *26, 28* Butler wrote of a trout, ' 'Tis with
a single hair pulled out'; and Dryden wrote of a woman who could 'draw you
to her with a single hair'.

Fair tresses man's imperial race insnare,
And beauty draws us with a single hair.
  Th' adventurous *Baron* the bright locks admired;
He saw, he wished, and to the prize aspired.   30
Resolved to win, he meditates the way,
By force to ravish, or by fraud betray;
For when success a lover's toil attends,
Few ask, if fraud or force attained his ends.
  For this, ere *Phœbus* rose, he had implored   35
Propitious Heaven, and ev'ry power adored:
But chiefly *Love*—to *Love* an altar built,
Of twelve vast *French* romances, neatly gilt.
There lay three garters, half a pair of gloves;
And all the trophies of his former loves.   40
With tender *billet-doux* he lights the pyre,
And breathes three am'rous sighs to raise the fire.
Then prostrate falls, and begs with ardent eyes
Soon to obtain, and long possess the prize:
The powers gave ear, and granted half his prayer,   45
The rest, the winds dispersed in empty air.
But now secure the painted vessel glides,
The sun-beams trembling on the floating tides,
While melting music steals upon the sky,
And softened sounds along the waters die.   50
Smooth flow the waves, the zephyrs gently play,
Belinda smiled, and all the world was gay.
All but the *Sylph*—with careful thoughts oppressed,
Th' impending woe sat heavy on his breast.
He summons straight his denizens of air;   55
The lucid squadrons round the sails repair:

27 alludes to the Greek story of Doris, who bound up her lover's hands with one hair 32 *fraud or force* a common choice in epic 45 *Aeneid* xi 759, 'Apollo heard, and granting half his prayer, Shuffled in winds the rest, and tossed in empty air' (Dryden 1144). 48 *floating tides* could mean 'high water'. 52 Pope's *Spring* 71, 'If Delia smiles, the flowers begin to spring'. 56 *lucid* bright; translucent; both meanings evoked in lines 61–2

Soft o'er the shrouds aerial whispers breathe,
That seemed but *Zephyrs* to the train beneath.
Some to the sun their insect-wings unfold,
Waft on the breeze, or sink in clouds of gold;   60
Transparent forms, too fine for mortal sight,
Their fluid bodies half dissolved in light.
Loose to the wind their airy garments flew,
Thin glitt'ring textures of the filmy dew,
Dipped in the richest tincture of the skies,   65
Where light disports in ever-mingling dyes;
While ev'ry beam new transient colours flings,
Colours that change whene'er they wave their wings.
Amid the circle on the gilded mast,
Superior by the head, was *Ariel* placed;   70
His purple pinions opening to the sun,
He raised his azure wand, and thus begun:
  'Ye *Sylphs* and *Sylphids*, to your chief give ear;
Fays, Fairies, Genii, Elves, and *Dæmons,* hear:
Ye know the spheres and various tasks assigned   75
By laws eternal to th' aerial kind.
Some in the fields of purest *Aether* play,
And bask and whiten in the blaze of day.
Some guide the course of wand'ring orbs on high,
Or roll the planets through the boundless sky.   80
Some less refined, beneath the moon's pale light
Pursue the stars that shoot athwart the night,
Or suck the mists in grosser air below,
Or dip their pinions in the painted bow,
Or brew fierce tempests on the wintry main,   85
Or o'er the glebe distil the kindly rain.
Others on earth o'er human race preside,
Watch all their ways, and all their actions guide:

---

58 train retinue *70–9* see *Paradise Lost* i 589, v 600, ii 528 ff. *73 sylphids* female
sylphs *76 aerial kind* seems here to include all the spirits just named

Of these the chief the care of nations own,
And guard with arms divine the *British Throne*.   90
    'Our humbler province is to tend the fair,
Not a less pleasing, though less glorious care.
To save the powder from too rude a gale,
Nor let th' imprisoned essences exhale;
To draw fresh colours from the vernal flowers;   95
To steal from rainbows, ere they drop in showers
A brighter wash; to curl their waving hairs,
Assist their blushes, and inspire their airs;
Nay oft, in dreams, invention we bestow,
To change a *Flounce*, or add a *Furbelow*.   100
    'This day, black omens threat the brightest fair
That e'er deserved a watchful spirit's care;
Some dire disaster, or by force, or slight;
But what, or where, the Fates have wrapped in night.
Whether the nymph shall break *Diana's* law,   105
Or some frail *China* jar receive a flaw;
Or stain her honour, or her new brocade,
Forget her prayers, or miss a masquerade,
Or lose her heart, or necklace, at a ball;
Or whether Heaven has doomed that *Shock* must fall.   110
Haste then ye spirits! to your charge repair;
The flutt'ring fan be *Zephyretta's* care;
The drops to thee, *Brillante*, we consign;
And, *Momentilla*, let the watch be thine;
Do thou, *Crispissa*, tend her fav'rite lock;   115
Ariel himself shall be the guard of *Shock*.
    'To fifty chosen *Sylphs*, of special note,
We trust th' important charge, the *petticoat*:

---

97 wash cosmetic wash *98 airs* stylish affectations (?) *100 furbelow* much the
same as a flounce; gathered strips of material *103 slight* = sleight; with pun?
113 drops diamonds ('brilliants') worn on the ear *115 Crispissa* from Latin
'crispo', curl

Oft have we known that seven-fold fence to fail,
Though stiff with hoops, and armed with ribs of whale.   120
Form a strong line about the silver bound,
And guard the wide circumference around.

   'Whatever spirit, careless of his charge,
His post neglects, or leaves the fair at large,
Shall feel sharp vengeance soon o'ertake his sins,   125
Be stopped in *vials*, or transfixed with *pins*;
Or plunged in lakes of bitter *washes* lie,
Or wedged whole ages in a *bodkin's* eye:
Gums and *pomatums* shall his flight restrain,
While clogged he beats his silken wings in vain;   130
Or alum *styptics* with contracting power
Shrink his thin essence like a rivelled flower.
Or, as *Ixion* fixed, the wretch shall feel
The giddy motion of the whirling mill,
In fumes of burning chocolate shall glow,   135
And tremble at the sea that froths below!'

   He spoke; the spirits from the sails descend;
Some, orb in orb, around the nymph extend,
Some thrid the mazy ringlets of her hair,
Some hang upon the pendants of her ear: 140
With beating hearts the dire event they wait,
Anxious, and trembling for the birth of Fate.

CANTO III

CLOSE by those meads, for ever crowned with flowers,
Where *Thames* with pride surveys his rising towers,
There stands a structure of majestic frame,
Which from the neighb'ring *Hampton* takes its name.

119 seven-fold fence like the seven-fold shield of Ajax *132 rivelled* shrunken and
wrinkled *133 Ixion* his presumption was punished by Zeus who bound him to a
wheel *134 mill* for grinding cocoa-seeds *138* see *Paradise Lost* v 596

Here *Britain's* statesmen oft the fall foredoom   5
Of foreign tyrants, and of nymphs at home;
Here thou, great *Anna!* whom three realms obey,
Dost sometimes counsel take—and sometimes *tea.*

  Hither the heroes and the nymphs resort,
To taste a while the pleasures of a court;   10
In various talk th' instructive hours they passed,
Who gave the *ball*, or paid the *visit* last:
One speaks the glory of the *British Queen*,
And one describes a charming *Indian screen*;
A third interprets motions, looks, and eyes;   15
At every word a reputation dies.
Snuff, or the *fan*, supply each pause of chat,
With singing, laughing, ogling, and all that.

  Meanwhile declining from the noon of day,
The sun obliquely shoots his burning ray;   20
The hungry judges soon the sentence sign,
And wretches hang that jurymen may dine;
The merchant from th' *exchange* returns in peace,
And the long labours of the *toilette* cease.
Belinda now, whom thirst of fame invites,
Burns to encounter two advent'rous knights,
At *ombre* singly to decide their doom;
And swells her breast with conquests yet to come.
Straight the three bands prepare in arms to join,
Each band the number of the sacred nine.   30
Soon as she spreads her hand, th' aeriel gaard
Descend, and sit on each important card:

---

7 three realms Great Britain, Ireland and France (to which the English crown still pretended) *17 snuff* a growing vogue in Anne's reign *18 and all that* Pope mimics the talkers *24* Dryden's *Aeneid* vii 171, 'And the long labours of your voyage end' *27 ombre* ('omber') played with nine cards per hand; Belinda as Ombre chooses trumps; she wins the first four tricks and loses the next four; by winning the last she avoids 'codille' and takes the game. Pope describes the Rouen Court cards, but many features are common.

First *Ariel* perched upon a *Matadore*,
Then each, according to the rank he bore;
For *Sylphs*, yet mindful of their ancient race,   35
Are, as when women, wondrous fond of place.

Behold, four *Kings* in majesty revered,
With hoary whiskers and a forky beard;
And four fair *Queens* whose hands sustain a flower,
Th' expressive emblem of their softer power;   40
Four *Knaves* in garbs succinct, a trusty band,
Caps on their heads, and halberts in their hand;
And parti-coloured troops, a shining train,
Draw forth to combat on the velvet plain.

The skilful nymph reviews her force with care: 45
'*Let Spades be trumps!*' she said, and trumps they were. *Belinda*
Now move to war her sable *Matadores*, *representing generic*
In show like leaders of the swarthy *Moors*, *woman - one of the*
Spadillio first, unconquerable lord! *ordering forces of the*
Led off two captive trumps, and swept the board. *world.*   50
As many more *Manillio* forced to yield,
And marched a victor from the verdant field.
Him *Basto* followed, but his fate more hard
Gained but one trump and one plebeian card.
With his broad sabre next, a chief in years,   55
The hoary Majesty of *Spades* appears,
Puts forth one manly leg, to sight revealed;
The rest, his many-coloured robe concealed.
The rebel *Knave*, who dares his prince engage,
Proves the just victim of his royal rage.   60
Ev'n mighty *Pam* that kings and queens o'erthrew,
And mowed down armies in the fights of *Lu*, *(or Loo)*

---

46 compare Genesis i 3 *47 Matadores* the three top trumps, named as Belinda
leads them *49 Spadillio* Ace of Spades *51 Manillio* two of trump suit *53 Basto*
Ace of Clubs *61 mighty Pam* Knave of Clubs, top card in Loo

Sad chance of war! now destitute of aid,
Falls undistinguished by the victor *Spade*!
   Thus far both armies to *Belinda* yield;   65
Now to the *Baron* fate inclines the field.
His warlike *Amazon* her host invades,
Th' imperial consort of the crown of *Spades*.
The *Club's* black tyrant first her victim died,
Spite of his haughty mien, and barb'rous pride: 70
What boots the regal circle on his head,
His giant limbs in state unwieldy spread?
That long behind he trails his pompous robe,
And of all monarchs only grasps the globe?
   The *Baron* now his *Diamonds* pours apace;   75
Th' embroidered *King* who shows but half his face,
And his refulgent *Queen*, with powers combined,
Of broken troops an easy conquest find.
Clubs, *Diamonds*, *Hearts*, in wild disorder seen,
With throngs promiscuous strow the level green.   80
Thus when dispersed a routed army runs,
Of *Asia's* troops, and *Afric's* sable sons,
With like confusion different nations fly,
Of various habit and of various dye,
The pierced battalions disunited fall,   85
In heaps on heaps; one fate o'erwhelms them all.
   The *Knave* of *Diamonds* tries his wily arts,
And wins (oh shameful chance!) the *Queen* of *Hearts*.
At this, the blood the virgin's cheek forsook,
A livid paleness spreads o'er all her look;
She sees, and trembles at th' approaching ill,
Just in the jaws of ruin, and *Codille*.   90
And now (as oft in some distempered state)
On one nice *Trick* depends the gen'ral fate.

64 Pope's *Iliad* xvi 776; Sarpedon 'Lies undistinguished from the vulgar dead
67 warlike Amazon Queen of Spades, last remaining trump

An *Ace* of Hearts steps forth: the *King* unseen 95
Lurked in her hand, and mourned his captive *Queen*.
He springs to vengeance with an eager pace,
And falls like thunder on the prostrate *Ace*.
The nymph exulting fills with shouts the sky,
The walls, the woods, and long canals reply. 100

O thoughtless mortals! ever blind to fate,
Too soon dejected, and too soon elate!
Sudden these honours shall be snatched away,
And cursed for ever this victorious day.

For lo! the board with cups and spoons is crowned, 105
The berries crackle, and the mill turns round.
On shining altars of *Japan* they raise
The silver lamp; the fiery spirits blaze.
From silver spouts the grateful liquors glide,
While *China's* earth receives the smoking tide. 110
At once they gratify their scent and taste,
And frequent cups prolong the rich repast.
Straight hover round the fair her airy band;
Some, as she sipped, the fuming liquor fanned,
Some o'er her lap their careful plumes displayed, 115
Trembling, and conscious of the rich brocade.
Coffee (which makes the politician wise,
And see through all things with his half-shut eyes)
Sent up in vapours to the *Baron's* brain
New stratagems, the radiant lock to gain. 120
Ah cease rash youth! desist ere 'tis too late,
Fear the just gods, and think of *Scylla's* fate!
Changed to a bird, and sent to flit in air,
She dearly pays for *Nisus'* injured hair!

95 the Ace of a red suit when not trumps rated three below the King *99–104* for
the classical echoes see headnote *106* the beans are roasted, then ground *107 altars
of Japan* lacquered tables *109 grateful* gratifying *110 China's earth* the cups *115
displayed* unfolded *117 politician* i.e. the amateur in the coffee house *122 Scylla.*
She plucked from the head of her father Nisus the purple hair on which his
kingdom's safety depended (Ovid *Met.* viii).

But when to mischief mortals bend their will,   125
How soon they find fit instruments of ill!
Just then, *Clarissa* drew with tempting grace
A two-edged weapon from her shining case:
So ladies in romance assist their knight,
Present the spear, and arm him for the fight.   130
He takes the gift with reverence, and extends
The little engine on his fingers' ends,
This just behind *Belinda's* neck he spread,
As o'er the fragrant steams she bends her head:
Swift to the lock a thousand sprights repair,   135
A thousand wings, by turns, blow back the hair,
And thrice they twitched the diamond in her ear,
Thrice she looked back, and thrice the foe drew near.
Just in that instant, anxious *Ariel* sought
The close recesses of the virgin's thought;   140
As on the nosegay in her breast reclined,
He watched th' ideas rising in her mind,
Sudden he viewed, in spite of all her art,
An earthly lover lurking at her heart.
Amazed, confused, he found his power expired,   145
Resigned to fate, and with a sigh retired.
    The peer now spreads the glitt'ring *Forfex* wide,
T' inclose the lock; now joins it, to divide.
Ev'n then, before the fatal engine closed,
A wretched *Sylph* too fondly interposed;   150
Fate urged the shears, and cut the *Sylph* in twain,
(But airy substance soon unites again)
The meeting points the sacred hair dissever
From the fair head, for ever and for ever!

132 engine word used in Pope's time for large or small contrivances *144 earthly
lover* his presence in her heart violates her chastity and thus disables Ariel (see
Dedication) *151–3* Pope's note compares 'Satan cut asunder by the Angel Michael'
(*Paradise Lost* vi 330)

Then flashed the living lightning from her eyes,　　　155
And screams of horror rend th' affrighted skies.
Not louder shrieks to pitying Heaven are cast,
When husbands or when lap-dogs breathe their last,
Or when rich *China* vessels, fall'n from high,
In glitt'ring dust and painted fragments lie!　　　160
　'Let wreaths of triumph now my temples twine,
(The victor cried) the glorious prize is mine!
While fish in streams, or birds delight in air,
Or in a coach and six the *British* fair,
As long as *Atalantis* shall be read,　　　165
Or the small pillow grace a lady's bed,
While *Visits* shall be paid on solemn days,
When numerous wax-lights in bright order blaze,
While nymphs take treats, or assignations give,
So long my honour, name, and praise shall live!'　　　170
What Time would spare, from steel receives its date,
And monuments, like men, submit to fate!
Steel could the labour of the gods destroy,
And strike to dust th' imperial towers of *Troy*;
Steel could the works of mortal pride confound,　　　175
And hew triumphal arches to the ground.
What wonder then, fair nymph! thy hairs should feel
The conquering force of unresisted steel?

CANTO IV

But anxious cares the pensive nymph oppressed,
And secret passions laboured in her breast.

165 Atalantis The New Atalantis, scandalous 'secret memoirs' by Mrs Manley
166 small pillow gracing a lady's counterpane as she received visitors in bed *167–8*
evening visits were formal with lights displayed as in a 'solemn' rite *178 unresisted
steel* recalling the epic sword or lance
1 Pope's note compares *Aeneid* iv 1; 'But anxious cares already seized the Queen'
(Dryden).

48

Not youthful kings in battle seized alive,
Not scornful virgins who their charms survive,
Not ardent lovers robbed of all their bliss,
Not ancient ladies when refused a kiss,   5
Not tyrants fierce that unrepenting die,
Not *Cynthia* when her *manteau's* pinned awry,
E'er felt such rage, resentment and despair,
As thou, sad virgin! for thy ravished hair.   10

For, that sad moment, when the *Sylphs* withdrew,
And *Ariel* weeping from *Belinda* flew,
Umbriel, a dusky melancholy spright,   *"the graver prude"*
As ever sullied the fair face of light,
Down to the central earth, his proper scene,   15
Repaired to search the gloomy Cave of *Spleen*.

Swift on his sooty pinions flits the *gnome*,
And in a vapour reached the dismal dome.
No cheerful breeze this sullen region knows,
The dreaded *east* is all the wind that blows.   20
Here in a grotto, sheltered close from air,
And screened in shades from day's detested glare,
She sighs for ever on her pensive bed,
Pain at her side, and *Megrim* at her head.

Two handmaids wait the throne: alike in place,   25
But diff'ring far in figure and in face.
Here stood *Ill-nature* like an ancient maid,
Her wrinkled form in black and white arrayed;
With store of prayers, for mornings, nights, and noons,
Her hand is filled; her bosom with lampoons.   30
There *Affectation* with a sickly mien,
Shows in her cheek the roses of eighteen,

---

8 *manteau* mantua, a loose gown *10 ravished hair* phrase used in Sandys's
translation of the Nisus story (see above III 125) *16 cave* see Ovid *Met.* ii, the
cave of Envy *spleen* fashionable term for melancholic ill-humour *18 vapour* cloud;
splenetic humour (see p. 287) *24 Megrim* migraine, treated here as an allegoric
figure *25 wait* attend *29* suggesting a rancorous piety (see *Spectator* 185) *30
lampoons* virulent personal satires

49

Practised to lisp, and hang the head aside,
Faints into airs, and languishes with pride,
On the rich quilt sinks with becoming woe,   35
Wrapped in a gown, for sickness, and for show.
The fair ones feel such maladies as these,
When each new night-dress gives a new disease.

A constant *vapour* o'er the palace flies;
Strange phantoms rising as the mists arise;   40
Dreadful, as hermits' dreams in haunted shades,
Or bright as visions of expiring maids.
Now glaring fiends, and snakes on rolling spires,
Pale spectres, gaping tombs, and purple fires:
Now lakes of liquid gold, Elysian scenes,   45
And crystal domes, and angels in machines.

Unnumbered throngs on every side are seen
Of bodies changed to various forms by *Spleen*.
Here living *tea-pots* stand, one arm held out,
One bent; the handle this, and that the spout: 50
A pipkin there, like *Homer's tripod* walks;
Here sighs a jar, and there a goose-pie talks;
Men prove with child, as powerful fancy works,
And maids turned bottles, call aloud for corks.

Safe passed the *Gnome* through this fantastic band,   55
A branch of healing *Spleen-wort* in his hand.
Then thus addressed the power: 'Hail, wayward Queen!
Who rule the sex to fifty from fifteen,
Parent of vapours and of female wit,
Who give th' *Hysteric* or *Poetic* fit;   60

41–6 compare Canto I 29–34 *43 spires* spirals *46 angels in machines* do the maids
confuse heaven with the theatre? *51 pipkin* small cooking pot *Homer's tripod*
Vulcan's walking tripods, Pope's *Iliad* xviii 440, *52 goose-pie* 'Alludes to a real
fact a Lady of distinction imagined herself in this condition' (Pope). *56 spleen-
wort* kind of fern; Aeneas in the underworld carried the golden bough. *57–78* like
Nisus to Luna, *Aeneid* ix 404 *a pimple* see p. 87 *60 fit* possibly with chime on
old meaning, 'stanza'

On various tempers act by various ways,
Make some take physic, others scribble plays;
Who cause the proud their visits to delay,
And send the godly in a pet, to pray;
A nymph there is, that all thy power disdains, *she doesn't really* 65
And thousands more in equal mirth maintains. *care about the rape,*
But oh! if e'er thy *Gnome* could spoil a grace, *but for her prudery.*
Or raise a pimple on a beauteous face, *see*
Like citron waters matrons' cheeks inflame,
Or change complexions at a losing game; 70
If e'er with airy horns I planted heads,
Or rumpled petticoats, or tumbled beds,
Or caused suspicion when no soul was rude,
Or discomposed the head-dress of a prude,
Or e'er to costive lap-dog gave disease, 75
Which not the tears of brightest eyes could ease:
Hear me, and touch *Belinda* with chagrin;
That single act gives half the world the spleen.'
    The Goddess with a discontented air
Seems to reject him, though she grants his prayer. 80
A wondrous bag with both her hands she binds,
Like that where once *Ulysses* held the winds;
There she collects the force of female lungs, *all forcefully*
Sighs, sobs, and passions, and the war of tongues. *applied – for show*
A vial next she fills with fainting fears, 85
Soft sorrows, melting griefs, and flowing tears.
The *Gnome* rejoicing bears her gifts away,
Spreads his black wings, and slowly mounts to day.
    Sunk in *Thalestris'* arms the nymph he found,
Her eyes dejected and her hair unbound. 90

---

69 citron waters brandy and lemon *74* i.e. to expose more of the prude's hair *80*
the Goddess has wonderfully pettish manners *82 Odyssey* x 19 *90* Dryden's
Aeneid iii 92, 'With eyes dejected, and with hair unbound' *90 dejected* cast
down

Full o'er their heads the swelling bag he rent,
And all the furies issued at the vent.
Belinda burns with more than mortal ire,
And fierce *Thalestris* fans the rising fire;
'O wretched maid!' she spread her hands, and cried,　　95
(While *Hampton's* echoes, 'Wretched maid!' replied)
'Was it for this you took such constant care
The *bodkin, comb,* and *essence* to prepare?
For this your locks in paper durance bound?
For this with tort'ring irons wreathed around?　　100
For this with fillets strained your tender head,
And bravely bore the double loads of lead?
Gods! shall the ravisher display your hair,
While the fops envy and the ladies stare!
Honour forbid! at whose unrivalled shrine　　105
Ease, pleasure, virtue, all, our sex resign.
Methinks already I your tears survey,
Already hear the horrid things they say,
Already see you a degraded toast,
And all your honour in a whisper lost!　　110
How shall I then your helpless fame defend?
'Twill then be infamy to seem your friend!
And shall this prize, th' inestimable prize,
Exposed through crystal to the gazing eyes,
And heightened by the diamond's circling rays,　　115
On that rapacious hand for ever blaze?
Sooner shall grass in *Hyde Park Circus* grow,
And wits take lodgings in the sound of *Bow;*
Sooner let earth, air, sea, to *Chaos* fall,
Men, monkeys, lap-dogs, parrots, perish all!　　120

95–120 like Nestor to the Greeks, *Iliad* vii 145 *98 bodkin* here a hair-pin *101
fillets* head-bands; sometimes worn in antiquity by sacrificial victims *102 loads of
lead* on curl-papers; on prisoners *105–6 honour* changes its meaning as different
qualities are resigned for it *108 horrid things* Pope mimics fashionable talk, but
it is an epic adjective. *109 degraded toast* deposed celebrity *Circus* see p. 94n.
118 sound of Bow i.e. in the City; wits lived in the West.

She said; then raging to *Sir Plume* repairs,
And bids her *Beau* demand the precious hairs:
(*Sir Plume* of *amber snuff-box* justly vain,
And the nice conduct of a *clouded cane*)
With earnest eyes, and round unthinking face,   125
He first the snuff-box opened, then the case,
And thus broke out—'My Lord, why, what the devil!
Z—ds! damn the lock! 'fore Gad, you must be civil!
Plague on't! 'tis past a jest—nay prithee, pox!
Give her the hair'—he spoke, and rapped his box.   130
   'It grieves me much (replied the peer again)
Who speaks so well should ever speak in vain,
But by this lock, this sacred lock, I swear,
(Which never more shall join its parted hair,
Which never more its honours shall renew,   135
Clipped from the lovely head where late it grew)
That while my nostrils draw the vital air,
This hand, which won it, shall for ever wear.'
He spoke, and speaking, in proud triumph spread
The long-contended honours of her head.   140
   But *Umbriel*, hateful *Gnome*! forbears not so;
He breaks the vial whence the sorrows flow.
Then see! the *Nymph* in beauteous grief appears,
Her eyes half-languishing, half-drowned in tears;
On her heaved bosom hung her drooping head,   145
Which, with a sigh, she raised; and thus she said:
   'For ever curs'd be this detested day,
Which snatched my best, my fav'rite curl away!
Happy! ah ten times happy, had I been,
If *Hampton Court* these eyes had never seen!   150

123 Sir Plume Sir George Browne, who resented the portrait *124 clouded*
variegated *128 z—ds* zounds *133 I swear* 'In allusion to Achilles's oath in
Homer' (Pope); *Iliad* i 309. *135 honours* Dryden's *Aeneid* x 172, 'And shook the
sacred honours of his head' *141 forbears not so* i.e. having burst the bag he does
not refrain from breaking the vial *147–67* like Achilles's lament for Patroclus,
Iliad xviii 107

Yet am I not the first mistaken maid,
By love of *Courts* to numerous ills betrayed.
Oh had I rather unadmired remained
In some lone isle, or distant northern land;
Where the gilt *chariot* never marks the way,   155
Where none learn *ombre*, none e'er taste *bohea*!
There kept my charms concealed from mortal eye,
Like roses that in deserts bloom and die.
What moved my mind with youthful lords to roam?
Oh had I stayed, and said my prayers at home!   160
'Twas this, the morning *omens* seemed to tell;
Thrice from my trembling hand the *patch-box* fell;
The tott'ring *China* shook without a wind;
Nay, *Poll* sat mute, and *Shock* was most unkind!
A *Sylph* too warned me of the threats of Fate,   165
In mystic visions, now believed too late!
See the poor remnants of these slighted hairs!
My hands shall rend what ev'n thy rapine spares:
These, in two sable ringlets taught to break,
Once gave new beauties to the snowy neck.   170
The sister-lock now sits uncouth, alone,
And in its fellow's fate foresees its own;
Uncurled it hangs, the fatal shears demands;
And tempts once more thy sacrilegious hands.
Oh hadst thou, cruel! been content to seize   175
Hairs less in sight, or any hairs but these!'

156 bohea a black tea *157–8* see Waller 'Go, lovely Rose', stanza 2 *176* what does honour mean now?

54

CANTO V

She said: the pitying audience melt in tears;
But *Fate* and *Jove* had stopped the *Baron*'s ears.
In vain *Thalestris* with reproach assails,
For who can move when fair *Belinda* fails?
Not half so fixed the *Trojan* could remain,   5
While *Anna* begged and *Dido* raged in vain.
Then grave *Clarissa* graceful waved her fan;
Silence ensued, and thus the nymph began:
  'Say, why are beauties praised and honoured most,
The wise man's passion, and the vain man's toast?   10
Why decked with all that land and sea afford?
Why angels called, and angel-like adored?
Why round our coaches crowd the white-gloved beaus?
Why bows the side-box from its inmost rows?
How vain are all these glories, all our pains,   15
Unless good sense preserve what beauty gains;
That men may say, when we the front-box grace,
"Behold the first in virtue as in face!"
Oh! if to dance all night, and dress all day,
Charmed the small-pox, or chased old age away;   20
Who would not scorn what housewife's cares produce,
Or who would learn one earthly thing of use?
To patch, nay, ogle, might become a saint,
Nor could it sure be such a sin to paint.
But since, alas! frail beauty must decay,   25
Curled or uncurled, since locks will turn to grey,
Since painted, or not painted, all shall fade,
And she who scorns a man, must die a maid;

1–2 Aeneid iv 440, Dryden 'Fate, and the God, had stopped his ears to love
(637) *9–34* Clarissa's speech was added in 1717 'to open more clearly the moral
of the poem, in a parody of the speech of Sarpedon to Glaucus in Homer'
(Pope); see *Iliad* xii 371 *14–18* gentlemen sat in the side, ladies in the front
boxes, with the young unmarried ladies in the first row

What then remains, but well our power to use, *the right*
And keep good-humour still whate'er we lose? *proportion* 30
And trust me, dear, good-humour can prevail, *(these are*
When airs, and flights, and screams, and scolding fail. *necessary, but*
Beauties in vain their pretty eyes may roll; *should not be*
Charms strike the sight, but merit wins the soul.' *prolonged)* 35

So spoke the dame, but no applause ensued;
Belinda frown'd, *Thalestris* call'd her prude.
'To arms, to arms!' the fierce virago cries,
And swift as lightning to the combat flies.
All side in parties, and begin th' attack;
Fans clap, silks rustle, and tough whalebones crack; 40
Heroes' and heroines' shouts confus'dly rise,
And bass, and treble voices strike the skies. *verbal conflict*
No common weapons in their hands are found, *(must keep*
Like Gods they fight, nor dread a mortal wound. *to their own*

So when bold *Homer* makes the Gods engage, *level of action* 45
And heavenly breasts with human passions rage; *level of action*
'Gainst *Pallas*, *Mars*; *Latona*, *Hermes* arms; *Cannot give to*
And all *Olympus* rings with loud alarms; *much concern in*
Jove's thunder roars, Heaven trembles all around; *reality)*
Blue *Neptune* storms, the bellowing deeps resound; 50
Earth shakes her nodding towers, the ground gives way;
And the pale ghosts start at the flash of day!

Triumphant *Umbriel* on a sconce's height
Clapped his glad wings, and sate to view the fight:
Propped on their bodkin spears, the sprights survey 55
The growing combat, or assist the fray.

While through the press enraged *Thalestris* flies,
And scatters death around from both her eyes,
A *beau* and *witling* perished in the throng,
One died in *metaphor*, and one in *song*. 60

35 'It is a verse frequently repeated in Homer after any speech: So spoke—and
all the heroes applauded' (Pope). *45 bold Homer* Pope cites *Iliad* xx 90 *52* finely
renders *Aeneid* viii 246 *53 sconce* firescreen; fortification

'O cruel nymph! a living death I bear,'
Cried *Dapperwit*, and sunk beside his chair.
A mournful glance *Sir Fopling* upwards cast,
'Those eyes are made so killing,'—was his last:
Thus on Meander's flowery margin lies   65
Th' expiring swan, and as he sings he dies.

    When bold *Sir Plume* had drawn *Clarissa* down,
Chloe stepp'd in, and killed him with a frown;
She smiled to see the doughty hero slain,
But, at her smile, the beau revived again.   70

    Now *Jove* suspends his golden scales in air,
Weighs the men's wits against the lady's hair;
The doubtful beam long nods from side to side;
At length the wits mount up, the hairs subside.

    See fierce *Belinda* on the *Baron* flies,   75
With more than usual lightning in her eyes:
Nor feared the chief th' unequal fight to try,
Who sought no more than on his foe to die.
But this bold lord, with manly strength endued,
She with one finger and a thumb subdued: 80
Just where the breath of life his nostrils drew,
A charge of *snuff* the wily virgin threw;
The *Gnomes* direct, to ev'ry atom just,
The pungent grains of titillating dust.
Sudden, with starting tears each eye o'erflows,   85
And the high dome re-echoes to his nose.

    'Now meet thy fate,' incensed *Belinda* cried,
And drew a deadly *bodkin* from her side.

---

62 Dapperwit character in Wycherley's *Love in a Wood 63 Sir Fopling* hero of Etheridge's *Man of Mode 64* from a song in the popular opera Camilla *69–70* renders Ovid *Ep.* vii 1 (quoted in Pope's note) *71–4* Pope cites *Iliad* viii 87 and *Aeneid* xii 725 *78 on his foe to die* puns on the Baron's ambitions as soldier and lover *81* see Canto IV 137 *86 dome* may also mean 'mansion' or 'sky' *88 bodkin* hairpin; dagger *88–96* 'In imitation of the progress of Agamemnon's sceptre in Homer' (Pope); see *Iliad* ii 129.

(The same, his ancient personage to deck,
Her great-great-grandsire wore about his neck, 90
In three *seal-rings*; which after, melted down,
Form'd a vast *buckle* for his widow's gown:
Her infant grandame's *whistle* next it grew,
The *bells* she jingled, and the *whistle* blew;
Then in a *bodkin* graced her mother's hairs, 95
Which long she wore, and now *Belinda* wears.)
　'Boast not my fall, (he cried) insulting foe!
Thou by some other shalt be laid as low.
Nor think to die dejects my lofty mind; *submitting to marriage*
All that I dread, is leaving you behind! 100
Rather than so, ah let me still survive,
And burn in *Cupid's* flames,—but burn alive.'
　'*Restore the lock!*' she cries; and all around
'*Restore the lock!*' the vaulted roofs rebound.
Not fierce *Othello* in so loud a strain 105
Roared for the handkerchief that caused his pain.
But see how oft ambitious aims are crossed,
And chiefs contend till all the prize is lost!
The lock, obtained with guilt, and kept with pain,
In every place is sought, but sought in vain: 110
With such a prize no mortal must be blest,
So Heaven decrees! with Heaven who can contest?
　Some thought it mounted to the lunar sphere,
Since all things lost on earth, are treasured there.
There heroes' wits are kept in pond'rous vases, 115
And beaus' in *snuff-boxes* and *tweezer-cases*.
There broken vows, and death-bed alms are found,
And lover's hearts with ends of riband bound;

113–22 Pope cites Ariosto, *Orlando Furioso* xxxiv 68 Astolfo finds on the moon,
'A mighty mass of things strangely confused Things that on earth were lost, or
were abused'. *115* On Ariosto's moon man's wit is kept in jars, because lost on
earth for love, ambition or vain causes. *116* Pope's refinement of Ariosto's jar
fantasy *117 death-bed alms* called 'fruitless' by Ariosto, and so implied here; why?

The courtier's promises, and sick man's prayers,
The smiles of harlots, and the tears of heirs,   120
Cages for gnats, and chains to yoke a flea,
Dried butterflies, and tomes of casuistry.

But trust the Muse—she saw it upward rise,
Though marked by none but quick poetic eyes:
(So *Rome's* great founder to the heavens withdrew,   125
To *Proculus* alone confessed in view)
A sudden star it shot through liquid air,
And drew behind a radiant *trail of hair*.
Not *Berenice's* locks first rose so bright,
The heavens bespangling with dishevelled light.   130
The *Sylphs* behold it kindling as it flies,
And pleased pursue its progress through the skies.

This the *beau-monde* shall from the *Mall* survey,
And hail with music its propitious ray.
This the blest lover shall for *Venus* take,   135
And send up vows from *Rosamonda's* Lake.
This *Partridge* soon shall view in cloudless skies,
When next he looks through *Galileo's* eyes;
And hence th' egregious wizard shall foredoom
The fate of *Louis*, and the fall of *Rome*.   140

Then cease, bright nymph! to mourn thy ravished hair
Which adds new glory to the shining sphere!
Not all the tresses that fair head can boast
Shall draw such envy as the lock you lost.

---

122 dried butterflies see p. 114 *casuistry* conscience-squaring apologetics *129 Berenice's lock* stolen by Jupiter from the temple of Venus and hung among the stars *133 the Mall* then an enclosed walk in St James's Park *136 Rosamonda's Lake* then in St James's Park; said to be 'long consecrated to disastrous love, and elegiac poetry' *137* 'John Partridge was a ridiculous Star-gazer, who in his Almanacks every year, never failed to predict the downfall of the Pope, and the King of France, then at war with the English' (Pope); his death was falsely predicted by Swift in the Bickerstaff Papers. *138 Galileo's eyes* his telescope

For, after all the murders of your eye,   *inevitable*   145
When, after millions slain, yourself shall die;
When those fair suns shall set, as set they must,
And all those tresses shall be laid in dust:
This lock, the Muse shall consecrate to fame,
And midst the stars inscribe *Belinda's* name.   150

Comparison with Berenice (but she volunteered to sacrifice hers to the goddess of love for the safe return of her husband).

*"Beauty is truth & t. is b.
That is all we know,
and all we need to know" Grecian Urn.

But the art in of life not enough"*

149-50 compareI 14, and Spenser, *Amoretti* 75

Elegy to the Memory of an Unfortunate Lady

AMONG Pope's earliest works was a translation of Ovid's *Sapphe to Phaon*, which opens:

> Say, lovely youth, that dost my heart command,
> Can *Phaon's* eyes forget his *Sappho's* hand?
> Must then her name the wretched writer prove?
> To thy remembrance lost, as to thy love!
> Ask not the cause that I new numbers chuse,
> The lute neglected, and the lyric muse;
> Love taught my tears in sadder notes to flow,
> And tuned my heart to elegies of woe.

If we dwell upon the *timbre* and mood of these lines we can see that *To the Memory of an Unfortunate Lady* and *Eloisa to Abelard* (published in the 1717 *Works*) are 'elegies of woe' that need not have had any occasion but a literary one. As refreshment from Homer Pope proved himself in the mode of Ovid's *Heroic Epistles*.

Nevertheless, there is some excuse for supposing that it was indeed love that taught Pope's tears to flow in sadder notes. We have reason to believe that at this time both Martha Blount and Lady Mary Wortley Montagu were particularly close to his affections. Yet the fact (if such it is) tells us nothing whatever about the poems.

Attempts to trace the lady out of the poem into actual life have, of course, been unsuccessful. Her rank, her love, her suffering at the hands of her family and her suicide among strangers are all as fictional as the ghost of the opening line. The story is ambiguous and obscure. We are told only what we need to know as occasions for the poet's pity, wonder, indication; for his anger, tenderness and irony. It has been said that the imprecations against the family are 'childish'. But it is not so. This is the consolatory wrath that belongs to the elegy—its springs are in compassion and it composes a tragic protest against the injustice that overtakes innocence. The wit of the poet is consolatory too—the metaphors of the first three paragraphs make the lady's death a privilege and, most movingly, a 'bright reversion', where a suggestion of return to a luminous and aetherial order plays upon the legal sense of 'deferred inheritance'. Yet what becomes of the poet's resources at the end of the poem?

The *Elegy* is discussed by F. R. Leavis in *Revaluation*, by Christopher Gillies in *Interpretations* edited by John Wain, and by R. A. Brower, *Pope: the Poetry of Allusion*. Dr Johnson says that 'Poetry has not often been worse employed than in dignifying the amorous fury of a raving girl'.

The typography here follows the 1717 edition.

ELEGY

TO THE MEMORY OF AN UNFORTUNATE LADY

WHAT beck'ning ghost, along the moonlight shade
Invites my step, and points to yonder glade?
'Tis she!—but why that bleeding bosom gored,
Why dimly gleams the visionary sword?
Oh ever beauteous, ever friendly! tell,   5
Is it, in heaven, a crime to love too well?
To bear too tender, or too firm a heart,
To act a Lover's or a *Roman's* part?

2 *step* Pope apparently revised 'steps', the 1717 reading. *8 Roman's part* suicide;
Cleopatra dies 'after the high Roman fashion'

Is there no bright reversion in the sky,
For those who greatly think, or bravely die?   10
      Why bade ye else, ye Powers! her soul aspire
Above the vulgar flight of low desire?
Ambition first sprung from your blest abodes,
The glorious fault of Angels and of Gods:
Thence to their Images on earth it flows,   15
And in the breasts of Kings and Heroes glows!
Most souls, 'tis true, but peep out once an age,
Dull sullen pris'ners in the body's cage:
Dim lights of life that burn a length of years,
Useless, unseen, as lamps in sepulchres;   20
Like Eastern Kings a lazy state they keep,
And close confined to their own palace sleep.
      From these perhaps (ere Nature bade her die)
Fate snatched her early to the pitying sky.
As into air the purer spirits flow,   25
And sep'rate from their kindred dregs below;
So flew the soul to its congenial place,
Nor left one virtue to redeem her Race.
      But thou, false guardian of a charge too good,
Thou, mean deserter of thy brother's blood!   30
See on these ruby lips the trembling breath,
These cheeks, now fading at the blast of death:
Cold is that breast which warmed the world before,
And those love-darting eyes must roll no more.
Thus, if eternal justice rules the ball,   35
Thus shall your wives, and thus your children fall:
On all the line a sudden vengeance waits,
And frequent hearses shall besiege your gates.

9 bright reversion see headnote *15 images* in Biblical sense (e.g. Gen. i 27) *18 the body's cage* a Platonic image *20 lamps in sepulchres* compare *E oisa,* l. 261 *21 lazy state* a pun *25 purer spirits* with pun on chemical sense, 'finer essences' *26 kindred dregs* chemical residue; the body once kin to the soul *28 race* family, kindred; or human race? *35 the ball* the orb, symbolizing the world, carried by figures of Justice

There passengers shall stand, and pointing say,
(While the long fun'rals blacken all the way,)   40
'Lo! these were they, whose souls the Furies steeled,
And cursed with hearts unknowing how to yield.'
Thus unlamented pass the proud away,
The gaze of fools, and pageant of a day!
So perish all, whose breast ne'er learned to glow   45
For others' good, or melt at others' woe.
    What can atone (oh ever-injured shade!)
Thy fate unpitied, and thy rites unpaid?
No friend's complaint, no kind domestic tear
Pleased thy pale ghost, or graced thy mournful bier;   50
By foreign hands thy dying eyes were closed,
By foreign hands thy decent limbs composed,
By foreign hands thy humble grave adorned,
By strangers honoured, and by strangers mourned!
What though no friends in sable weeds appear,   55
Grieve for an hour, perhaps, then mourn a year,
And bear about the mockery of woe
To midnight dances, and the public show?
What, though no weeping Loves thy ashes grace,
Nor polished marble emulate thy face?   60
What though no sacred earth allow thee room,
Nor hallowed dirge be muttered o'er thy tomb?
Yet shall thy grave with rising flowers be dressed,
And the green turf lie lightly on thy breast:
There shall the morn her earliest tears bestow,   65
There the first roses of the year shall blow;
While angels with their silver wings o'ershade
The ground, now sacred by thy reliques made.
    So peaceful rests, without a stone, a name,
What once had beauty, titles, wealth, and fame.   70
How loved, how honoured once, avails thee not,
To whom related, or by whom begot;

39 passengers passers by *52 decent* comely

A heap of dust alone remains of thee;
'Tis all thou art, and all the proud shall be!
    Poets themselves must fall, like those they sung;   75
Deaf the praised ear, and mute the tuneful tongue.
Even he, whose soul now melts in mournful lays,
Shall shortly want the gen'rous tear he pays;
Then from his closing eyes thy form shall part,
And the last pang shall tear thee from his heart,   80
Life's idle business at one gasp be o'er,
The Muse forgot, and thou belov'd no more!

78 want lack; need *tear* sometimes used for 'elegy'

Eloisa to Abelard

Eloisa to Abelard is more obviously in the tradition of the Heroic Epistle than the *Elegy to the Memory of an Unfortunate Lady*. But the tradition had not slept before Pope's time. It had flourished in France and in England throughout the seventeenth century. So too had the love-letter as a literary form, with many of the qualities of the essay meant for a wide public, but keeping something of the immediacy and intimacy of the true letter. Among the finest of performances of this kind are the *Five Love-Letters from a Nun to a Cavalier*, translated into English by Roger L'Estrange in 1678. But immediately behind Pope's poem are the letters of Eloisa to Abelard as translated from the French by John Hughes and published in 1713.

Abelard (1079–1142) was the foremost scholar and disputant of his generation. When nearly forty he fell in love with Eloisa, the eighteen-year-old daughter of Fulbert, canon of Paris Cathedral. A secret marriage temporarily appeased Fulbert's anger when the affair was discovered to him, but Abelard found himself obliged later to admit Eloisa to the nunnery of Argenteuil near Paris. Fulbert persisted in his persecution and hired thugs to break into Abelard's lodgings and emasculate him. After a period of retirement Abelard resumed his writing and teaching and founded a convent dedicated to the Paraclete (a name for the Comforter or Holy Spirit), and it was here that Eloisa and others of her community took refuge when they were expelled from Argenteuil. It is said that Eloisa read by chance a letter in which

Abelard comforted a friend by relating his own misfortunes, and this began the correspondence between them.

It is essential that this poem, like the *Elegy*, be read aloud. It has a theatrical, larger-than-life quality that is kept consistent with restraint and literary decorum. There is much to remind us that control of movement is control of emotion. Yet the skills that control are also those that intensify and release:

> Thy life a long-dead calm of fixed repose;
> No pulse that riots, and no blood that glows.
> Still as the sea, ere winds were taught to blow,
> Or moving spirit bade the waters flow.

Saintliness is associated with pain and immobility and coldness, with the unmoved and silent statues of the chapel. Life belongs to letters:

> They live, they speak, they breathe what love inspires,
> Warm from the soul, and faithful to its fires.

and to those relics of sped love: Name, Idea and Fame. Here, as in the *Elegy*, it is words that must triumph over distress. There is a rhetoric of love and a rhetoric of renunciation, but both meet in the several moments of the poem when religious and erotic feeling mix. The simple word 'mixed' is one of a number which take on a special intensity:

> Hide it, my heart, within that close disguise,
> Where, mixed with God's, his loved idea lies.
> (11–12)

> And here, ev'n then, shall my cold dust remain,
> Here all its frailties, all its flames resign,
> And wait til 'tis no sin to mix with thine.
> (174—6)

But the 'mixing' of different kinds of feeling takes place all the time; from, for example, the mixed pride and despair of:

> Still rebel nature holds out half my heart.   (26)

to that gathering of passion into beatitude of:

> Where flames refined in breasts seraphic glow.   (320)

The poem moves in a tradition that looks back through Crashaw to the *Song of Solomon*—poetry of divine wedding:

> For her th'unfading rose of Eden blooms,
> And wings of seraphs shed divine perfumes;
> (216–17)

But Pope does not share Crashaw's unabashed readiness to identify the rival kinds of rapture. He feels the mysterious likenesses, tensions and paradoxes:

> Ev'n here, where frozen chastity retires,
> Love finds an altar for forbidden fires.
> (181–2)

Pope again makes moving use of his experience in pastoral poetry —the artificial diction that recaptures the fragile serenity of certain charmed states of mind:

> The dying gales that pant upon the trees,
> The lakes that quiver to the curling breeze;
> No more these scenes my meditation aid,
> Or lull to rest the visionary maid.
>
> (159–62)

But more striking is his use of the 'Gothick' and 'Romantic' modes, touching the 'browner horror on the woods' and returning us to the echoing vaults from which the poem's mood first springs.

The debt to Hughes is considerable, and the history of the translation and the poem would show that masterpieces are the work of many imaginations over many generations. Pope is not inventing but perfecting. Hughes, for example, following his French copy, often expresses warmth of passion in an imagery of fire, burning and flowing blood. His Eloisa writes:

When we love pleasures, we love the living, and not the dead. We leave off burning with desire for those who can no longer burn for us. This was my cruel uncle's notion.

From this pathetic, elegantly turned sentiment Pope created an emblem:

The torch of Venus burns not for the dead.

This has a monumental, symbolic quality perfectly consonant with the mood of the poem; formal but intense; flame extinguished into stone.

The same intensifications might be observed in other transformations of Hughes's prose. Here, for instance, is the source passage behind 225–34:

After having passed the day in thinking of you, full of the dear idea, I give myself up at night to sleep: then it is that Heloise, who dares not without trembling think of you by day, resigns herself entirely to the pleasure of hearing you, and speaking to you. I see you Abelard, and glut my eyes with the sight; sometimes you entertain me with the story of your secret troubles and grievances, and create in me a sensible sorrow; sometimes, forgetting the perpetual obstacles to our desires, you press me to make you happy, and I easily yield to your transports. Sleep gives you what your enemies' rage has deprived you of; and our souls, animated with the same passion, are sensible of the same pleasure. But, oh! ye delightful illusions, soft errors, how soon do you vanish away! At my awaking I open my eyes and see no Abelard; I stretch out my arm to take hold of him, but he is not there; I call him, he hears me not.

Pope's version is charged with doublenesses of feeling and meaning:

> O curst, dear horror of all-conscious night!
> How glowing guilt exalts the keen delight!

The intensity of the verse and of the experience (actual and literary) which has fashioned it, is clear in a comparison with Pope's early translation of Ovid's *Sappho to Phaon*:

> O night more pleasing than the brightest day,
> When Fancy gives what Absence takes away,
> And drest in all its visionary charms,
> Restores my fair deserter to my arms!

The few glimpses of Hughes's version given in the notes to this edition are meant to suggest the direction of Pope's refining and perfecting, and sometimes they explain obscurities in the text.

For further reading see the Twickenham Edition (ed. Tillotson) and R. A. Brower, *Pope: the Poetry of Allusion*. For an interesting Victorian attack on the poem see the Rev. Whitwell Elvin's edition in the 1871 *Works*. Dr Johnson, however, calls *Eloisa* 'one of the most happy productions of human wit'. That Pope found the writing of the poem personally congenial is suggested by allusions to it in letters to Martha Blount and Lady Montagu; the end of the poem may be meant for either or both these ladies, but it is in any case an appropriate ending.

The punctuation, capitalization and italicization follow the 1717 edition.

ELOISA TO ABELARD

In these deep solitudes and awful cells,
Where heavenly-pensive contemplation dwells;
And ever-musing melancholy reigns;
What means this tumult in a Vestal's veins?
Why rove my thoughts beyond this last retreat?   5
Why feels my heart its long-forgotten heat?
Yet, yet I love!—From *Abelard* it came,
And *Eloisa* yet must kiss the name.

   Dear fatal name! rest ever unrevealed,
Nor pass these lips in holy silence sealed.   10
Hide it, my heart, within that close disguise,
Where, mixed with God's, his loved Idea lies.
Oh write it not, my hand—the name appears
Already written—wash it out, my tears!
In vain lost *Eloisa* weeps and prays,   15
Her heart still dictates, and her hand obeys.

   Relentless walls! whose darksome round contains
Repentant sighs, and voluntary pains:
Ye rugged rocks! which holy knees have worn;
Ye grots and caverns shagged with horrid thorn!   20
Shrines! where their vigils pale-eyed virgins keep,
And pitying saints, whose statues learn to weep!
Though cold like you, unmoved, and silent grown,
I have not yet forgot myself to stone.
All is not Heaven's while *Abelard* has part,   25
Still rebel nature holds out half my heart;
Nor prayers nor fasts its stubborn pulse restrain,
Nor tears, for ages, taught to flow in vain.

---

1 awful awe-inspiring *4–6* Abelard writes: 'My passion still lives in me; the fire
is only covered with deceitful ashes, and cannot be extinguished but by extraordinary grace.' *20 horrid* bristling *22 learn to weep* alluding to moisture on
cold stone

Soon as thy letters trembling I unclose,
That well-known name awakens all my woes.   30
Oh name for ever sad! for ever dear!
Still breathed in sighs, still ushered with a tear.
I tremble too, where'er my own I find,
Some dire misfortune follows close behind.
Line after line my gushing eyes o'erflow,   35
Led through a sad variety of woe:
Now warm in love, now with'ring in my bloom,
Lost in a convent's solitary gloom!
There stern religion quenched th' unwilling flame,
There died the best of passions, Love and Fame.   40

  Yet write, oh write me all, that I may join
Griefs to thy griefs, and echo sighs to thine:
Nor foes nor fortune take this power away.
And is my *Abelard* less kind than they?
Tears still are mine, and those I need not spare,   45
Love but demands what else were shed in prayer;
No happier task these faded eyes pursue,
To read and weep is all they now can do.

  Then share thy pain, allow that sad relief;
Ah more than share it! give me all thy grief.   50
Heaven first taught letters for some wretch's aid,
Some banished lover, or some captive maid;
They live, they speak, they breathe what love inspires,
Warm from the soul, and faithful to its fires,
The virgin's wish without her fears impart,   55
Excuse the blush, and pour out all the heart,
Speed the soft intercourse from soul to soul,
And waft a sigh from *Indus* to the *Pole*.

30–34 Eloisa writes: 'I met with my name a hundred times; I never saw it
without fear; some heavy calamity always followed it: I saw yours too, equally
unhappy.' *40 Fame* Hughes says Abelard was 'ardent in the pursuit of fame',
while the wit and learning of Eloisa were such that 'her fame began to spread
itself abroad'.

Thou know'st how guiltless first I met thy flame,
When Love approach'd me under Friendship's name;   60
My fancy form'd thee of Angelic kind,
Some emanation of th' all-beauteous Mind.
Those smiling eyes, attemp'ring ev'ry ray,
Shone sweetly lambent with celestial day:
Guiltless I gazed; Heaven listened while you sung;   65
And truths divine came mended from that tongue.
From lips like those what precept failed to move?
Too soon they taught me 'twas no sin to love.
Back through the paths of pleasing sense I ran,
Nor wish'd an Angel whom I loved a Man.   70
Dim and remote the joys of saints I see;
Nor envy them, that heaven I lose for thee.
    How oft, when pressed to marriage, have I said,
Curse on all laws but those which love has made!
Love, free as air, at sight of human ties,   75
Spreads his light wings, and in a moment flies.
Let wealth, let honour, wait the wedded dame,
August her deed, and sacred be her fame;
Before true passion all those views remove,
Fame, wealth, and honour! what are you to Love?   80
The jealous God, when we profane his fires,
Those restless passions in revenge inspires;
And bids them make mistaken mortals groan,
Who seek in love for aught but love alone.
Should at my feet the world's great master fall,   85
Himself, his throne, his world, I'd scorn 'em all:

59–72 compare Donne, *Air and Angels* *62 emanation* a flowing-forth of the
divine *63 attempering* controlling and assuaging the divine fire and light *64
lambent* 'shining with a soft clear light and without fierce heat' (O.E.D.) *66
mended* made whole again; made better *73–90* Eloisa writes: 'Though I knew
that the name of wife was honourable in the world, and holy in religion, yet
the name of your mistress had greater charms because it was more free.' *81
jealous God* Eros; but Abelard writes: 'Why provoke a jealous God with
blasphemy?'

Not *Cæsar's* empress would I deign to prove;
No, make me mistress to the man I love;
If there be yet another name more free,
More fond than mistress, make me that to thee!   90
Oh happy state! when souls each other draw,
When love is liberty, and nature law:
All then is full, possessing, and possessed,
No craving Void left aching in the breast:
Even thought meets thought ere from the lips it part,   95
And each warm wish springs mutual from the heart.
This sure is bliss (if bliss on earth there be)
And once the lot of *Abelard* and me.

    Alas, how changed! what sudden horrors rise!
A naked lover bound and bleeding lies!   100
Where, where was *Eloise?* her voice, her hand,
Her poniard, had opposed the dire command.
Barbarian stay! that bloody stroke restrain;
The crime was common, common be the pain.
I can no more; by shame, by rage suppressed,   105
Let tears, and burning blushes speak the rest.

    Canst thou forget that sad, that solemn day,
When victims at yon altar's foot we lay?
Canst thou forget what tears that moment fell,
When, warm in youth, I bade the world farewell?   110
As with cold lips I kissed the sacred veil,
The shrines all tremblèd, and the lamps grew pale:
Heaven scarce believed the conquest it surveyed,
And Saints with wonder heard the vows I made.
Yet then, to those dread altars as I drew,   115
Not on the Cross my eyes were fixed, but you:
Not grace, or zeal, love only was my call,
And if I lose thy love, I lose my all.

104 pain punishment *107 solemn day* i.e. of Eloisa's profession of vows; with a
glance at the 'sacrifice' just described? *108 victims* Abelard attended Eloisa's
profession.

Come! with thy looks, thy words, relieve my woe;
Those still at least are left thee to bestow.   120
Still on that breast enamoured let me lie,
Still drink delicious poison from thy eye,
Pant on thy lip, and to thy heart be pressed;
Give all thou canst—and let me dream the rest.
Ah no! instruct me other joys to prize,   125
With other beauties charm my partial eyes,
Full in my view set all the bright abode,
And make my soul quit *Abelard* for God.

   Ah, think at least thy flock deserves thy care,
Plants of thy hand, and children of thy prayer.   130
From the false world in early youth they fled,
By thee to mountains, wilds, and deserts led.
You raised these hallowed walls; the desert smiled,
And Paradise was opened in the Wild.
No weeping orphan saw his father's stores   135
Our shrines irradiate, or emblaze the floors;
No silver saints, by dying misers given,
Here bribed the rage of ill-requited heaven:
But such plain roofs as piety could raise,
And only vocal with the Maker's praise.   140
In these lone walls (their day's eternal bound)
These moss-grown domes with spiry turrets crowned,
Where awful arches make a noon-day night,
And the dim windows shed a solemn light;
Thy eyes diffused a reconciling ray,   145
And gleams of glory brightened all the day.

125–8 Eloisa writes: 'Without changing the ardour of our affections, let us change their object.' *133–7* Abelard founded the convent, which owed nothing to rich patronage. *134* see Isaiah li 3, *Paradise Lost* iv 131 *136 irradiate* make bright with ornament *emblaze* make glowing *141 their day's eternal bound* a complex phrase suggesting timelessness, dedication, aspiration and confinement, each differently stressed in the next five lines; perhaps, 'each day within them is contained in the eternal'

But now no face divine contentment wears,
'Tis all blank sadness, or continual tears.
See how the force of others' prayers I try,
(O pious fraud of am'rous charity!)   150
But why should I on others' prayers depend?
Come thou, my father, brother, husband, friend!
Ah let thy handmaid, sister, daughter move,
And, all those tender names in one, thy love!
The darksome pines that o'er yon rocks reclined   155
Wave high, and murmur to the hollow wind,
The wand'ring streams that shine between the hills,
The grots that echo to the tinkling rills,
The dying gales that pant upon the trees,
The lakes that quiver to the curling breeze;   160
No more these scenes my meditation aid,
Or lull to rest the visionary maid:
But o'er the twilight groves, and dusky caves,
Long-sounding aisles, and intermingled graves,
Black Melancholy sits, and round her throws   165
A death-like silence, and a dread repose:
Her gloomy presence saddens all the scene,
Shades ev'ry flower, and darkens ev'ry green,
Deepens the murmur of the falling floods,
And breathes a browner horror on the woods.   170
   Yet here for ever, ever must I stay;
Sad proof how well a lover can obey!
Death, only death, can break the lasting chain;
And here even then, shall my cold dust remain,
Here all its frailties, all its flames resign,   175
And wait, till 'tis no sin to mix with thine.

---

152 Eloisa inscribes her first letter: 'To her Lord, her Father, her Husband, her Brother.' *162 visonary* seeing visions; seen in a vision *176* Abelard writes: 'I hope you will be contented . . . to be buried near me. Your cold ashes need then fear nothing.'

Ah wretch! believed the spouse of God in vain,
Confessed within the slave of love and man.
Assist me Heaven! but whence arose that prayer?
Sprung it from piety, or from despair?   180
Even here, where frozen chastity retires,
Love finds an altar for forbidden fires.
I ought to grieve, but cannot what I ought;
I mourn the lover, not lament the fault;
I view my crime, but kindle at the view,   185
Repent old pleasures, and solicit new:
Now turned to Heaven, I weep my past offence,
Now think of thee, and curse my innocence.
Of all affliction taught a lover yet,
'Tis sure the hardest science to forget!   190
How shall I lose the sin, yet keep the sense,
And love the offender, yet detest th' offence?
How the dear object from the crime remove,
Or how distinguish penitence from love?
Unequal task! a passion to resign,   195
For hearts so touched, so pierced, so lost as mine.
Ere such a soul regains its peaceful state,
How often must it love, how often hate!
How often hope, despair, resent, regret,
Conceal, disdain,—do all things but forget.   200
But let heaven seize it, all at once 'tis fired;
Not touched, but rapt; not wakened, but inspired!
Oh come! oh teach me nature to subdue,
Renounce my love, my life, myself—and you.
Fill my fond heart with God alone, for He   205
Alone can rival, can succeed to thee.

---

178 confessed with hint of religious sense *180 despair* by Catholic doctrine, a sin *189 affliction* either the subject or the indirect object of 'taught' *191 sense* perhaps 'the pleasures of sin', with a hint of 'understanding' *202* Eloisa writes of God and great men: 'When he pleases to touch them he ravishes them, and suffers them not to speak or breathe but for his glory.'

How happy is the blameless Vestal's lot!
The world forgetting, by the world forgot:
Eternal sunshine of the spotless mind!
Each prayer accepted, and each wish resigned;   210
Labour and rest, that equal periods keep;
'Obedient slumbers that can wake and weep';
Desires composed, affections ever even;
Tears that delight, and sighs that waft to Heaven.
Grace shines around her with serenest beams,   215
And whisp'ring Angels prompt her golden dreams.
For her th' unfading rose of *Eden* blooms,
And wings of Seraphs shed divine perfumes;
For her the Spouse prepares the bridal ring,
For her white virgins *Hymeneals* sing;   220
To sounds of heavenly harps, she dies away,
And melts in visions of eternal day.
    Far other dreams my erring soul employ,
Far other raptures, of unholy joy:
When at the close of each sad, sorrowing day,   225
Fancy restores what vengeance snatched away,
Then conscience sleeps, and leaving nature free,
All my loose soul unbounded springs to thee.
O cursed, dear horrors of all-conscious night!
How glowing guilt exalts the keen delight!   230
Provoking Dæmons all restraint remove,
And stir within me ev'ry source of love.
I hear thee, view thee, gaze o'er all thy charms,
And round thy phantom glue my clasping arms.
I wake—no more I hear, no more I view,   235
The phantom flies me, as unkind as you.

---

212 from Crashaw, *Of a Religious House* 225–34 a passage very close to
Hughes; see headnote *229 cursed* evil; ill-fated, *dear* grievous; precious *horrors*
shudders; thrills *all-conscious* applied to the night, 'all-knowing'; applied to the
lovers' sensation, 'fully known and shared', from Latin 'conscius'

I call aloud; it hears not what I say;
I stretch my empty arms; it glides away:
To dream once more I close my willing eyes;
Ye soft illusions, dear deceits, arise!   240
Alas, no more!—methinks we wand'ring go
Through dreary wastes, and weep each other's woe;
Where round some mould'ring tower pale ivy creeps,
And low-browed rocks hang nodding o'er the deeps.
Sudden you mount! you beckon from the skies;   245
Clouds interpose, waves roar, and winds arise.
I shriek, start up, the same sad prospect find,
And wake to all the griefs I left behind.

    For thee the fates, severely kind, ordain
A cool suspense from pleasure and from pain;   250
Thy life a long, dead calm of fixed repose;
No pulse that riots, and no blood that glows.
Still as the sea, ere winds were taught to blow,
Or moving spirit bade the waters flow;
Soft as the slumbers of a saint forgiven,   255
And mild as opening gleams of promised Heaven.

    Come, *Abelard*! for what hast thou to dread?
The torch of *Venus* burns not for the dead;
Nature stands check'd; religion disapproves:
Ev'n thou art cold—yet *Eloisa* loves.   260
Ah hopeless, lasting flames! like those that burn
To light the dead, and warm th' unfruitful urn.

    What scenes appear where'er I turn my view!
The dear ideas, where I fly, pursue,

249–52 Eloisa writes: 'Your misfortune has been the occasion of your finding
rest ... God, who seemed to lay his hand heavily upon you, sought only to help
you ... I am a thousand times more to be lamented than you ... I must resist
those fires which love kindles in a young heart.' *257* Eloisa writes: 'You may
see me ... without incurring any danger, since you can only relieve me with tears
and words.' *torch of Venus* see headnote *261 lasting flames* fires kept in ancient
tombs

Rise in the grove, before the altar rise,   265
Stain all my soul, and wanton in my eyes!
I waste the Matin lamp in sighs for thee,
Thy image steals between my God and me,
Thy voice I seem in ev'ry hymn to hear,
With ev'ry bead I drop too soft a tear.   270
When from the censer clouds of fragrance roll,
And swelling organs lift the rising soul,
One thought of thee puts all the pomp to flight,
Priests, Tapers, Temples, swim before my sight:
In seas of flame my plunging soul is drowned,   275
While altars blaze, and Angels tremble round.

While prostrate here in humble grief I lie,
Kind, virtuous drops just gath'ring in my eye,
While praying, trembling, in the dust I roll,
And dawning grace is opening on my soul: 280
Come, if thou dar'st, all charming as thou art!
Oppose thyself to Heaven; dispute my heart;
Come, with one glance of those deluding eyes
Blot out each bright Idea of the skies;
Take back that grace, those sorrows, and those tears,   285
Take back my fruitless penitence and prayers,
Snatch me, just mounting, from the bless'd abode,
Assist the Fiends and tear me from my God!
No, fly me, fly me! far as Pole from Pole;
Rise *Alps* between us! and whole oceans roll!   290
Ah come not, write not, think not once of me,
Nor share one pang of all I felt for thee.
Thy oaths I quit, thy memory resign,

266 stain colour; taint *wanton* play amorously, with hint of 'waste' *270 too soft*
i.e. from love, not repentance *281 all charming* Abelard writes: 'Could a virtuous
lady resist a man that had confounded all the learned of the age?' *282 dispute*
engage in formal disputation about *289 fly me* Abelard writes: 'Let me remove
far from you, and obey the apostle who said, Fly.' *293 quit* acquit; Abelard
writes: 'It will always be the highest love to shew none: I here release you of all
your oaths, and engagements.'

Forget, renounce me, hate whate'er was mine.
Fair eyes, and tempting looks, (which yet I view!)   295
Long loved, adored ideas! all adieu!
O grace serene! O virtue heavenly fair!
Divine oblivion of low-thoughted care!
Fresh blooming hope, gay daughter of the sky!
And faith, our early immortality!   300
Enter, each mild, each amicable guest;
Receive, and wrap me in eternal rest!
   See in her Cell sad *Eloisa* spread,
Propped on some tomb, a neighbour of the dead!
In each low wind methinks a Spirit calls,   305
And more than Echoes talk along the walls.
Here, as I watch'd the dying lamps around,
From yonder shrine I heard a hollow sound.
'Come, sister, come! (it said, or seemed to say)
Thy place is here, sad sister come away!   310
Once like thyself, I trembled, wept, and prayed,
Love's victim then, though now a sainted maid:
But all is calm in this eternal sleep;
Here grief forgets to groan, and love to weep,
Even superstition loses ev'ry fear: 315
For God, not man, absolves our frailties here.'
   I come, I come! prepare your roseate bow'rs,
Celestial palms, and ever-blooming flow'rs.
Thither, where sinners may have rest, I go,
Where flames refined in breasts seraphic glow.   320
Thou, *Abelard*! the last sad office pay,
And smooth my passage to the realms of day:
See my lips tremble, and my eye-balls roll,
Suck my last breath, and catch my flying soul!

---

315 superstition fear of the unknown *321–8* Eloisa writes: 'Is it not your part to
receive my last sighs, take care of my funeral, and give an account of my manners
and faith?'

Ah no—in sacred vestments may'st thou stand,   325
The hallow'd taper trembling in thy hand,
Present the Cross before my lifted eye,
Teach me at once, and learn of me to die.
Ah then, thy once-loved *Eloisa* see!
It will be then no crime to gaze on me.   330
See from my cheek the transient roses fly!
See the last sparkle languish in my eye!
Till ev'ry motion, pulse, and breath be o'er;
And ev'n my *Abelard* be loved no more.
O death all-eloquent! you only prove   335
What dust we dote on, when 'tis man we love.

     Then too, when fate shall thy fair frame destroy,
(That cause of all my guilt, and all my joy)
In trance ecstatic may thy pangs be drowned,
Bright clouds descend, and Angels watch thee round,   340
From opening skies may streaming glories shine,
And Saints embrace thee with a love like mine.

     May one kind grave unite each hapless name,
And graft my love immortal on thy fame.
Then, ages hence, when all my woes are o'er,   345
When this rebellious heart shall beat no more;
If ever chance two wand'ring lovers brings
To *Paraclete's* white walls, and silver springs,
O'er the pale marble shall they join their heads,
And drink the falling tears each other sheds;   350
Then sadly say, with mutual pity moved,
'Oh may we never love as these have loved!'
From the full choir when loud *Hosannas* rise,
And swell the pomp of dreadful sacrifice,

---

336 Abelard writes: 'You shall see me, to strengthen your piety by the horror of this carcase; and my death then, more eloquent than I can be, will tell you what you love when you love a man.' *343* Pope notes: 'Abelard and Eloisa were interred in the same grave, or in monuments adjoining, in the Monastery of the Paraclete.'

Amid that scene, if some relenting eye   355
Glance on the stone where our cold relics lie,
Devotion's self shall steal a thought from Heaven,
One human tear shall drop, and be forgiven.
And sure if fate some future Bard shall join,
In sad similitude of griefs to mine,   360
Condemn'd whole years in absence to deplore,
And image charms he must behold no more;
Such if there be, who love so long, so well;
Let him our sad, our tender story tell;
The well-sung woes will soothe my pensive ghost;   365
He best can paint 'em, who shall feel 'em most.

Epistles to Several Persons (Moral Essays)

POPE planned a great work which was to be completed in four books. The first of these, treating of man in the abstract, was finished in four epistles and published as *The Essay on Man*. The second, meant also for four parts, was to be about the intellectual capacities of man, but only some satirical fragments were written and these were incorporated into *The Dunciad*. The third book was to be in the form of an epic about Brutus, legendary Trojan founder of Britain, and was to treat of man in his social, political and religious capacities, but only a few lines were sketched in execution. The fourth book, about ethics or practical morality, was to be 'of many members', among them the four Epistles sometimes known as the Moral Essays, of which three are printed here. The Epistle omitted here is the 'First', 'To Lord Cobham, Of the Knowledge and Characters of Men'. The order of the Epistles accords with the scheme of the proposed great work. *To Cobham* is a sophisticated and sceptical account of the difficulties of 'reading' and studying men; *To a Lady* may be thought a complementary piece on women, but it is in fact more concerned with characteristics and is much less abstract; *To Bathurst* is predominantly about avarice and *To Burlington* about prodigality, the two intemperate extreme attitudes to wealth which lie either side of the golden mean. But the order of writing and publication was almost precisely the reverse, i.e. IV, III, I, II, with II possibly composed before I.

Epistle II To a Lady: Of the Characters of Women
This was finished in February 1733 and the 'Lady' to whom it
was addressed was Martha Blount who had, says Pope in a letter,
'the great modesty to insist on my suppressing her name'. In the
first edition (1735) Pope was able in an advertisement prefixed to
the poem to declare on his honour that 'no one character is drawn
from the life'; but in the last version he approved in his lifetime
Pope added the characters of Philomedé, Atossa and Chloe, and
these leave a keen impression of touching people closely. As far
as the reader of the satire is concerned, however, the *impression* of
truth to life matters more than the facts. The facts belong to the
history not of literature but of gossip.

But gossip has its own fascination, and even where the truth is
hard to reach, the findings and speculations about Pope's
characters have thrown much light on the social ethos, and on
the tempers and manners that made it what it was. Certain traits
of Philomedé were drawn from Henrietta, Duchess of Marlborough (died 1733) and certain of Chloe's from Pope's friend,
Mrs Howard, Countess of Suffolk, though in neither case can we
be sure that anything like an 'identification' was intended; in
defining feminine characteristics with wit and precision, Pope
had little choice but to enlist the women he knew. The Atossa
portrait is more complicated, since contemporary gossip had it
that Sarah, Duchess of Marlborough, paid Pope £1000 to suppress
it and that Pope failed to keep his part of the bargain. The origins
of the gossip, however, are obscure and testify to the malice
operating against Pope rather than to his own capacity for
treachery and blackmail. George Sherburn and F. W. Bateson
have argued that Katherine Darnley, Duchess of Buckinghamshire, fits the Atossa bill far better than the Duchess of Marlborough, and this opinion is likely to prevail.

Whatever their validity as actual cases, the 'characters' are
superb *exempla*, feats of deft moral analysis. The poem has
its distinct pastoral strain (see Introduction, pp. 12–15) with
the perverse energies of Atossa doing most to threaten the

composure cherished by the Lady (Martha Blount) in 'well-timed retreat'.

See F. W. Bateson (Twickenham edition); William Empson, *Seven Types of Ambiguity*; R. J. Allen, 'Pope and the Sister Arts', in *Pope and his Contemporaries* ed. Clifford and Landa (1949).

The typography is slightly simplified from that of 1744.

EPISTLE II

TO A LADY

OF THE CHARACTERS OF WOMEN

NOTHING so true as what you once let fall,
'Most Women have no Characters at all.'
Matter too soft a lasting mark to bear,
And best distinguished by black, brown, or fair.
   How many pictures of one Nymph we view,   5
All how unlike each other, all how true!
Arcadia's Countess, here, in ermined pride,
Is there, Pastora by a fountain side:
Here Fannia, leering on her own good man,
And there, a naked Leda with a Swan.   10
Let then the Fair one beautifully cry
In Magdalen's loose hair and lifted eye,
Or dressed in smiles of sweet Cecilia shine,
With simp'ring Angels, Palms, and Harps divine;
Whether the Charmer sinner it, or saint it,   15
If Folly grow romantic, I must paint it.

---

7 Arcadia's Countess Margaret Sawyer* *9 Fannia* type-name for an adultress; hence her leer and her Leda pose *12 Magdalen* identified with the 'sinner' who washed Jesus's feet with her hair (Luke vii 37) *loose hair and lifted eye* signifying humility and adoration, but with other insinuations

Come then, the colours and the ground prepare!
Dip in the Rainbow, trick her off in Air;
Choose a firm cloud, before it fall, and in it
Catch, ere she change, the Cynthia of this minute.   20
    Rufa, whose eye quick glancing o'er the Park,
Attracts each light gay meteor of a Spark,
Agrees as ill with Rufa studying Locke,
As Sappho's diamonds with her dirty smock,
Or Sappho at her toilet's greasy task,   25
With Sappho fragrant at an evening Mask:
So morning Insects that in muck begun,
Shine, buzz, and fly-blow in the setting sun.
    How soft is Silia! fearful to offend,
The Frail one's advocate, the Weak one's friend.   30
To her, Calista proved her conduct nice;
And good Simplicius asks of her advice.
Sudden, she storms! she raves! You tip the wink,
But spare your censure; Silia does not drink.
All eyes may see from what the change arose,   35
All eyes may see—a Pimple on her nose.
    Papillia, wedded to her doating spark,
Sighs for the shades—'How charming is a Park!'
A Park is purchased, but the Fair he sees
All bathed in tears—'Oh odious, odious Trees!'   40
    Ladies, like variegated Tulips, show,
'Tis to their Changes half their charms we owe;
Their happy Spots the nice admirer take,
Fine by defect, and delicately weak.
'Twas thus Calypso once each heart alarmed,   45
Awed without Virtue, without Beauty charmed;

---

21 Rufa a red-head *22 spark* dandy, with pun on 'meteor' *24 Sappho* for Lady
Montagu* *31 Calista* after the heroine of Rowe's Fair Penitent *31 nice* correct
37 Papillia from the Latin for butterfly *doating* some editions, 'amorous' *43–4*
couplet reversed in some editions *44 nice admirer take* attract the discriminating
45 Calypso after the goddess who charmed Ulysses

Her Tongue bewitch'd as oddly as her Eyes,
Less Wit than Mimic, more a Wit than wise;
Strange graces still, and stranger flights she had,
Was just not ugly, and was just not mad;   50
Yet ne'er so sure our passion to create,
As when she touch'd the brink of all we hate.
   Narcissa's nature, tolerably mild,
To make a wash would hardly stew a child,
Has even been proved to grant a Lover's prayer,   55
And paid a Tradesman once to make him stare;
Gave alms at Easter, in a Christian trim,
And made a Widow happy, for a whim.
Why then declare Good-nature is her scorn,
When 'tis by that alone she can be borne?   60
Why pique all mortals, yet affect a name?
A fool to Pleasure, yet a slave to Fame:
Now deep in Taylor and the Book of Martyrs,
Now drinking citron with his Grace and Chartres:
Now Conscience chills her, and now Passion burns;   65
And Atheism and Religion take their turns;
A very Heathen in the carnal part,
Yet still a sad, good Christian at her heart.
   See Sin in State, majestically drunk,
Proud as a Peeress, prouder as a Punk;   70
Chaste to her Husband, frank to all beside,
A teeming Mistress, but a barren Bride.
What then? let Blood and Body bear the fault,
Her Head's untouched, that noble Seat of Thought:
Such this day's doctrine—in another fit   75
She sins with Poets through pure Love of Wit.

---

53 Narcissa see headnote *54 wash* for the hair or cosmetic use *57 trim* manner
59 i.e. 'why then does she declare . . . ?' *61 affect a name* i.e. court a reputation,
like other mortals *62 fame* good repute; Jeremy Taylor's theme in *Holy Living
and Holy Dying*, and Foxe's in the *Book of Martyrs 64 citron* brandy and lemon
70 punk prostitute *75 fit* mood

What has not fired her bosom or her brain?
Cæsar and Tall-boy, Charles and Charlemagne.
As Helluo, late Dictator of the Feast,
The Nose of hautgout and the Tip of Taste,   80
Critiqued your wine, and analyzed your meat,
Yet on plain Pudding deigned at home to eat:
So Philomedé, lect'ring all mankind
On the soft Passion, and the Taste refined,
Th' Address, the Delicacy—stoops at once,   85
And makes her hearty meal upon a Dunce.

    Flavia's a Wit, has too much sense to Pray;
To Toast our wants and wishes is her way;
Nor asks of God, but of her stars, to give
The mighty blessing, 'while we live, to live.'   90
Then all for Death, that Opiate of the soul!
Lucretia's dagger, Rosamonda's bowl.
Say, what can cause such impotence of mind?
A Spark too fickle, or a Spouse too kind.
Wise Wretch! with Pleasures too refined to please;   95
With too much Spirit to be e'er at ease;
With too much Quickness ever to be taught;
With too much Thinking to have common Thought;
You purchase Pain with all that Joy can give,
And die of nothing but a Rage to live.   100

    Turn then from Wits; and look on Simo's Mate,
No Ass so meek, no Ass so obstinate.
Or her that owns her Faults, but never mends,
Because she's honest, and the best of Friends.
Or her whose life the Church and Scandal share,   105
For ever in a Passion, or a Prayer.

Or her who laughs at Hell, but (like her Grace)
Cries, 'Ah! how charming if there's no such place!'
Or who in sweet vicissitude appears
Of Mirth and Opium, Ratafie and Tears,   110
The daily Anodyne, and nightly Draught,
To kill those foes to Fair ones, Time and Thought.
Woman and Fool are two hard things to hit;
For true No-meaning puzzles more than Wit.
    But what are these to great Atossa's mind?   115
Scarce once herself, by turns all Womankind!
Who, with herself, or others, from her birth
Finds all her life one warfare upon earth:
Shines in exposing Knaves and painting Fools,
Yet is, whate'er she hates and ridicules.   120
No Thought advances, but her Eddy Brain
Whisks it about, and down it goes again.
Full sixty years the World has been her Trade,
The wisest Fool much Time has ever made.
From loveless youth to unrespected age,   125
No Passion gratified except her Rage,
So much the fury still outran the wit,
The Pleasure missed her, and the Scandal hit.
Who breaks with her, provokes Revenge from Hell,
But he's a bolder man who dares be well.   130
Her every turn with Violence pursued,
No more a storm her Hate than Gratitude:
To that each Passion turns, or soon or late;
Love, if it makes her yield, must make her hate.
Superiors? death! and Equals? what a curse!   135
But an Inferior not dependant? worse.
Offend her, and she knows not to forgive;
Oblige her, and she'll hate you while you live:

107 her Grace a duchess *110 ratafie* peach brandy *115 Atossa* a follower of
Sappho; here for Katherine Darnley* *130 be well* on good terms *133 to that* i.e.
to 'storm'

But die, and she'll adore you—then the Bust
And Temple rise—then fall again to dust.   140
Last night, her Lord was all that's good and great;
A Knave this morning, and his Will a Cheat.
Strange! by the Means defeated of the Ends,
By Spirit robbed of Power, by Warmth of Friends,
By Wealth of Followers! without one distress,   145
Sick of herself, through very selfishness!
Atossa, cursed with ev'ry granted prayer,
Childless with all her Children, wants an Heir.
To Heirs unknown descends the unguarded store,
Or wanders, Heaven-directed, to the Poor.   150

    Pictures like these, dear Madam, to design,
Ask no firm hand, and no unerring line;
Some wand'ring touch, or some reflected light,
Some flying stroke alone can hit 'em right:
For how should equal Colours do the knack?   155
Chameleons who can paint in white and black?

    'Yet Chloe sure was formed without a spot.—'
Nature in her then erred not, but forgot.
'With every pleasing, ev'ry prudent part,
Say, what can Chloe want?'—She wants a Heart.   160
She speaks, behaves, and acts, just as she ought,
But never, never, reached one gen'rous thought.
Virtue she finds too painful an endeavour,
Content to dwell in Decencies for ever.
So very reasonable, so unmoved,   165
As never yet to love, or to be loved.

---

140 fall again because not properly maintained *144 spirit* excessive determination *warmth* passion *145 distress* physical affliction *148* her children died before she did. *153 touch* some editions read 'touches, some' *155 equal* matched to the subject; equable *156 chameleons* perhaps, 'painters who exactly reflect the colours in front of them' *white and black* perhaps suggesting precise draftsmanship and hinting that these are the true colours of Atossa *157 Chloe* a glance at Henrietta Howard?* *164 decencies* proprieties

She, while her lover pants upon her breast,
Can mark the figures on an Indian chest;
And when she sees her Friend in deep despair,
Observes how much a Chintz exceeds Mohair!   170
Forbid it, Heaven, a Favour or a Debt
She e'er should cancel—but she may forget.
Safe is your Secret still in Chloe's ear;
But none of Chloe's shall you ever hear.
Of all her Dears she never slandered one,   175
But cares not if a thousand are undone.
Would Chloe know if you're alive or dead?
She bids her Footman put it in her head.
Chloe is prudent—would you too be wise?
Then never break your heart when Chloe dies.   180

One certain Portrait may (I grant) be seen,
Which Heaven has varnish'd out, and made a *Queen*:
The same for ever! and described by all
With Truth and Goodness, as with Crown and Ball.
Poets heap Virtues, Painters Gems at will,   185
And show their zeal, and hide their want of skill.
'Tis well—but, Artists! who can paint or write,
To draw the Naked is your true delight:
That Robe of Quality so struts and swells,
None see what Parts of Nature it conceals.   190
The exactest traits of Body or of Mind,
We owe to models of an humble kind.
If *Queensberry* to strip there's no compelling,
'Tis from a Handmaid we must take a Helen.
From Peer or Bishop 'tis no easy thing   195
To draw the man who loves his God or King:

---

168 mark the figures inspect the ornament *182 varnished out* tricked out; glossed over *Queen* Caroline *187 artists* i.e. those painters and poets who do not lack skill *190 parts of nature* includes the meaning 'natural abilities' *193 Queensberry* a Duchess, remarkable for her beauty

Alas! I copy (or my draught would fail)
From honest Mah'met, or plain Parson Hale.
   But grant, in Public, Men sometimes are shown,
A Woman's seen in Private life alone: 200
Our bolder Talents in full light displayed;
Your Virtues open fairest in the shade.
Bred to disguise, in Public 'tis you hide;
There, none distinguish 'twixt your Shame or Pride,
Weakness or Delicacy; all so nice,   205
That each may seem a Virtue or a Vice.
   In Men, we various Ruling Passions find;
In Women, two almost divide the kind;
Those, only fixed, they first or last obey,
The Love of Pleasure, and the Love of Sway.   210
   That, Nature gives; and where the lesson taught
Is still to please, can Pleasure seem a fault?
Experience, this; by Man's oppression cursed,
They seek the second not to lose the first.
   Men, some to Business, some to Pleasure take;   215
But every Woman is at heart a Rake:
Men, some to Quiet, some to public Strife;
But every Lady would be Queen for life.
   Yet mark the fate of a whole Sex of Queens!
Power all their end, but Beauty all the means: 220
In Youth they conquer with so wild a rage,
As leaves them scarce a Subject in their Age:
For foreign glory, foreign joy, they roam;
No thought of Peace or Happiness at home.
But Wisdom's Triumph is well-timed Retreat,   225
As hard a science to the Fair as Great!
Beauties, like Tyrants, old and friendless grown,
Yet hate to rest, and dread to be alone,

---

198 Mahomet nickname for a Turkish servant to George I *Parson Hale* Stephen Hales* *205 nice* coy *228 to rest* some editions 'repose'

Worn out in public, weary ev'ry eye,
Nor leave one sigh behind them when they die.   230
   Pleasures the sex, as children birds, pursue,
Still out of reach, yet never out of view,
Sure, if they catch, to spoil the Toy at most,
To covet flying, and regret when lost:
At last, to follies Youth could scarce defend,   235
It grows their Age's prudence to pretend;
Ashamed to own they gave delight before,
Reduced to feign it, when they give no more:
As Hags hold Sabbaths, less for joy than spite,
So these their merry, miserable Night;   240
Still round and round the Ghosts of Beauty glide,
And haunt the places where their Honour died.
   See how the World its Veterans rewards!
A youth of frolics, an old Age of Cards;
Fair to no purpose, artful to no end,   245
Young without Lovers, old without a Friend;
A Fop their Passion, but their Prize a Sot,
Alive, ridiculous, and dead, forgot!
   Ah, Friend! to dazzle let the Vain design;
To raise the Thought and touch the Heart, be thine!   250
That Charm shall grow, while what fatigues the Ring,
Flaunts and goes down, an unregarded thing.
So when the Sun's broad beam has tired the sight,
All mild ascends the Moon's more sober light,
Serene in Virgin Modesty she shines,   255
And unobserved the glaring Orb declines.
   Oh! blest with Temper, whose unclouded ray
Can make to-morrow cheerful as to-day;

---

239 sabbaths witches' sabbaths, annual orgies *240–1* evoke both the ballroom
and the gyrations of hags *251 the Ring* clump of trees in Hyde Park, round which
fashionable people used to drive; in hinting that charm so flaunted tires the
sight of the trees Pope recalls Virgil's 'silvas fatigant'. *257 temper* moderation,
self-control

She who can love a Sister's charms, or hear
Sighs for a Daughter with unwounded ear;   260
She, who ne'er answers till a Husband cools,
Or, if she rules him, never shows she rules;
Charms by accepting, by submitting sways,
Yet has her humour most, when she obeys;
Let Fops or Fortune fly which way they will;   265
Disdains all loss of Tickets, or Codille;
Spleen, Vapours, or Small-pox, above them all,
And Mistress of herself, though China fall.

   And yet, believe me, good as well as ill,
Woman's at best a Contradiction still.   270
Heaven, when it strives to polish all it can
Its last best work, but forms a softer Man;
Picks from each sex, to make the Fav'rite blest,
Your love of Pleasure, our desire of Rest:
Blends, in exception to all general rules,   275
Your Taste of Follies, with our Scorn of Fools,
Reserve with Frankness, Art with Truth allied,
Courage with Softness, Modesty with Pride,
Fix'd Principles, with Fancy ever new;
Shakes all together, and produces—You!   280
   Be this a Woman's Fame: with this unblest,
Toasts live a scorn, and Queens may die a jest.
This Phœbus promised (I forget the year)
When those blue eyes first opened on the sphere;
Ascendant Phœbus watched that hour with care,   285
Averted half your Parents' simple Prayer;

---

260 *sighs* ardent desires *unwounded* i.e. by envy 264 *humour* way; whim 266
tickets lottery tickets *codille* see p. 43n. 267 *spleen, vapours* ill-temper and depres-
sion caused by bad 'humours', exhalations from the organs of the body 281 i.e.
let her have certain qualities, not others 282 *Toasts* reigning belles *a scorn* to be
made mock of 283 *forget the year* Martha Blount was forty-four 284 *sphere* world,
with hint of cosmic sphere

And gave you Beauty, but denied the Pelf
That buys your sex a Tyrant o'er itself.
The gen'rous god, who Wit and Gold refines,
And ripens Spirits as he ripens Mines,   290
Kept Dross for Duchesses, the world shall know it,
To you gave Sense, Good humour, and a Poet.

Epistle III To Allen, Lord Bathurst: Of the Use of Riches
This was started in 1730 and published in 1733. It is a highly
wrought poem of which Pope said: 'I never took more care in my
life of anything.' The present text follows F. W. Bateson
(Twickenham edition) in respect to its line order, which is that of
1735. Warburton, possibly with Pope's consent, made a number
of alterations in sequence and cast the whole into a dialogue;
his version was as follows (all line references are to the present
text):

(a) 27–8 omitted.
(b) after 202 adds from MS, 'Yet sure, of qualities deserving
    praise/More go to ruin fortunes, than to raise.'
(c) 37–8 placed to follow 34.
(d) 65–78 placed to follow 38.
(e) '*P.*' (for Pope) inserted before 1, 23, 32, 34, 81, 82 (after
    'more?', 113, 237, 279, 285, 339. '*B.*' (for Bathurst) before
    21, 31, 33, 80 (after 'you'), 82 (after 'clothes'), 113, 229,
    275, 283, 338 (after 'tale').

The part given to Bathurst was absurdly small, and he very
rightly grumbled about the later editions.

Sherburn called the piece a 'caustic and partizan indictment of
Whig monied interest', and it is true that its victims are mostly
Whigs and its positives favour a paternal, simple country-house
rule. But the indictment of monied society is powerful in a line

287 *pelf* 'filthy lucre', devaluing the 'simple prayer' for prosperity 289 *wit and
gold refines* as god of poetry Phoebus purified wit, and as sun-god condensed
gold from the earth, leaving the 'dross' of 291

which reaches at least as far back as *Timon of Athens* (Timon's soliloquies should be read in this connection) and as far forward as R. H. Tawney's *The Acquisitive Society*. Pope in no way dishonours the models, from Virgil to the Book of Job, that are the ground of his imitations. He writes as heir at once to Horace and the Old Testament, and as mentor to Crabbe and Dickens.

The texture of the irony is very close, as in the central lines (169–236) about the distribution of wealth. In this couplet we feel that from one point of view (the insect's) it is an excellent thing that wealth should be freely released, but from another we know that riches like flies are a pest:

> Riches, like insects, when concealed they lie,
> Wait but for wings, and in their season, fly.

And the equivocations run on, crossing auspicious with malicious observation, through:

> In lavish streams to quench a Country's thirst,
> And men and dogs shall drink him till they burst.

until the problem is provisionally resolved in the metaphors of lines 233–7.

In a letter to Caryll Pope said of this Epistle: 'I shall make living examples, which enforce best, and consequently put you once more on the defence of your friend, against the roar and calumny which I expect, and am ready to suffer in so good a cause.' But the living examples are for the most part re-made into fictions of immense power.

EPISTLE III

TO ALLEN, LORD BATHURST

OF THE USE OF RICHES

Who shall decide, when Doctors disagree,
And soundest Casuists doubt, like you and me?
You hold the word, from Jove to Momus given,
That Man was made the standing jest of Heaven:
And Gold but sent to keep the fools in play,   5
For some to heap, and some to throw away.

But I, who think more highly of our kind
(And surely, Heaven and I are of a mind)
Opine, that Nature, as in duty bound,
Deep hid the shining mischief underground: 10
But when by Man's audacious labour won,
Flamed forth this rival to its sire, the Sun,
Then careful Heaven supplied two sorts of Men,
To squander these, and those to hide again.

Like Doctors thus, when much dispute has passed,   15
We find our tenets just the same at last.
Both fairly owning, Riches, in effect,
No grace of Heaven or token of th' Elect;
Given to the Fool, the Mad, the Vain, the Evil,
To Ward, to Waters, Chartres, and the Devil.   20
What Nature wants, commodious Gold bestows,
'Tis thus we eat the bread another sows:
But how unequal it bestows, observe,
'Tis thus we riot, while who sow it, starve:

---

2 *soundest casuists* men who try most honestly to square their consciences in matters of belief 3 *Jove, Momus* gods who despised man; Momus was the apotheosis of criticism 12 *its sire* the sun was thought to refine gold from the earth 20 *Waters* Walters*

98

What Nature wants (a phrase I much distrust) 25
Extends to Luxury, extends to Lust:
And if we count among the Needs of life
Another's Toil, why not another's Wife?
Useful, I grant, it serves what life requires,
But dreadful, too, the dark Assassin hires. 30
Trade it may help, Society extend:
But lures the Pirate, and corrupts the Friend.
It raises Armies in a Nation's aid:
But Bribes a Senate, and the Land's betray'd.
    Oh! that such bulky Bribes as all might see, 35
Still, as of old, incumbered Villainy!
In vain may Heroes fight, and Patriots rave;
If secret Gold saps on from knave to knave.
Could France or Rome divert our brave designs,
With all their brandies, or with all their wines? 40
What could they more than Knights and Squires confound,
Or water all the Quorum ten miles round?
A Statesman's slumbers how this speech would spoil!
'Sir, Spain has sent a thousand jars of oil;
Huge bales of British cloth blockade the door: 45
A hundred oxen at your levée roar.'
    Poor Avarice one torment more would find;
Nor could Profusion squander all in kind.
Astride his cheese Sir Morgan might we meet,
And Worldly crying coals from street to street, 50
Whom, with a wig so wild, and mien so mazed,
Pity mistakes for some poor tradesman crazed.
Had Colepepper's whole wealth been hops and hogs,
Could he himself have sent it to the dogs?
His Grace will game: to White's a Bull be led, 55

25 *wants* 'lacks' in 21; pun in 25 *27–8* omitted in 1751 'for their bad reasoning'
35 bulky bribes consignments of goods under the barter system 'of old' *42 water*
i.e. steep in liquor *quorum* Justices of the Peace *46 levée* morning assembly *49*
Morgan 'a fictitious name' (Pope) *55 White's* club in St James's Street

With spurning heels and with a butting head.
To White's be carried, as to ancient games,
Fair Coursers, Vases, and alluring Dames.
Shall then Uxorio, if the stakes he sweep,
Bear home six Whores, and make his Lady weep? 60
Or soft Adonis, so perfumed and fine,
Drive to St. James's a whole herd of swine?
Oh filthy check on all industrious skill,
To spoil the nation's last great trade, Quadrille!

    Once, we confess, beneath the Patriot's cloak, 65
From the crack'd bag the dropping Guinea spoke,
And jingling down the back-stairs, told the crew,
'Old Cato is as great a Rogue as you.'
Blest paper-credit! last and best supply!
That lends Corruption lighter wings to fly! 70
Gold imped by thee, can compass hardest things,
Can pocket States, can fetch or carry Kings;
A single leaf shall waft an Army o'er,
Or ship off Senates to some distant Shore;
A leaf, like Sibyl's, scatter to and fro 75
Our fates and fortunes, as the winds shall blow:
Pregnant with thousands flits the Scrap unseen,
And silent sells a King, or buys a Queen,

    Since then, my Lord, on such a World we fall,
What say you? 'Say? Why, take it, Gold and all.' 80

    What riches give us, let us then enquire:
Meat, Fire, and Clothes. What more? Meat, Clothes, and Fire.
Is this too little? would you more than live?
Alas! 'tis more than Turner finds they give.

59 Uxorio from uxurious *64 Quadrille* a card game *65 Patriot* a Tory; here
Christopher Musgrave, whose bag of guineas, a 'bulky bribe' from William III,
burst as he left the back door. *71 imped* strengthened in flight; from falconry
practice of grafting feather splints into damaged wings *75–6* from Dryden's
Aeneid vi 116, where Aeneas asks the Sybil not to prophecy to leaves 'Lest they
disperse in air our empty fate'. *84 Turner* an avaricious merchant, nicknamed
'Plum'

Alas! 'tis more than (all his visions past)   85
Unhappy Wharton, waking, found at last!
What can they give? to dying Hopkins Heirs;
To Chartres, Vigour; Japhet, Nose and Ears?
Can they in gems bid pallid Hippia glow,
In Fulvia's buckle ease the throbs below;   90
Or heal, old Narses, thy obscener ail,
With all th' embroidery plastered at thy tail?
They might (were Harpax not too wise to spend)
Give Harpax' self the blessing of a Friend;
Or find some Doctor that would save the life   95
Of wretched Shylock, spite of Shylock's Wife:
But thousands die, without or this or that,
Die, and endow a College, or a Cat.
To some indeed, Heaven grants the happier fate,
To enrich a Bastard, or a Son they hate.   100
     Perhaps you think the Poor might have their part?
Bond damns the Poor, and hates them from his heart:
The grave Sir Gilbert holds it for a rule
That 'every man in want is knave or fool':
'God cannot love (says Blunt, with tearless eyes)   105
The wretch he starves'—and piously denies:
But the good Bishop, with a meeker air,
Admits, and leaves them, Providence's care.
     Yet, to be just to these poor men of pelf,
Each does but hate his Neighbour as himself: 110

87 Hopkins nicknamed 'Vulture'; died exulting in a will which disinherited his kin for a generation *88 Japhet* Crook* *89 Hippia* from hippiatric, a horse-doctor or horse-leech; hence rapacious person *91 Narses* a Roman general, for Cadogan,* with pun on 'tail' *93 Harpax* Greek for robber *95–6* the dying miser could have a doctor if his wife would afford it. *97 without or this or that* deprived of money by death after living without its blessings *98 endow . . . a cat* Pope's note hints at a Duchess of Richmond, probably playfully. *102 Bond* met criticism of a swindling Charity of which he was director with, 'Damn the poor'. *103 Sir Gilbert* Heathcote*

Damn'd to the Mines, an equal fate betides
The slave that digs it, and the Slave that hides.
Who suffer thus, mere Charity should own,
Must act on motives powerful, though unknown.
Some War, some Plague, or Famine, they foresee,   115
Some Revelation hid from you and me.
Why Shylock wants a meal, the cause is found,
He thinks a Loaf will rise to fifty pound.
What made Directors cheat in South-sea year?
To live on ven'son when it sold so dear.   120
Ask you why Phryne the whole Auction buys?
Phryne foresees a general Excise.
Why she and Sappho raise that monstrous sum?
Alas! they fear a man will cost a plum.

   Wise Peter sees the World's respect for Gold,   125
And therefore hopes this Nation may be sold:
Glorious Ambition! Peter, swell thy store,
And be what Rome's great Didius was before.

   The crown of Poland, venal twice an age,
To just three millions stinted modest Gage.   130
But nobler scenes Maria's dreams unfold,
Hereditary Realms, and worlds of Gold.
Congenial souls! whose life one Av'rice joins,
And one fate buries in th' Asturian mines.

   Much-injured Blunt! why bears he Britain's hate?   135
A wizard told him in these words our fate:
'At length corruption, like a general flood
(So long by watchful Ministers withstood),

111 damned to the mines Roman punishment and phrase, 'damnare in metallum'
117 Shylock here Douglas* *121 Phryne* Greek courtesan; here Maria Skerret,
Walpole's mistress and in a position to know his tax proposals *123 Sappho* for
Lady Montagu* *124 plum* slang for £100,000 *127 Peter* Walter* *128 Didius*
rich Roman lawyer; he bought the Empire in A.D. 193 *129 venal* the electors of
the Polish king were open to bribery *130 Gage* an adventurer who bid
£3,000,000 for the Polish crown before going to work gold-mines in Spain;
there he met Mary Herbert ('Maria'), impoverished by her search for a royal
husband, and married her. *135 Blunt* a South Sea Company director

Shall deluge all; and Av'rice creeping on,
Spread like a low-born mist, and blot the Sun;   140
Statesman and Patriot ply alike the stocks,
Peeress and Butler share alike the Box,
And Judges job, and Bishops bite the town,
And mighty Dukes pack cards for half-a-crown.
See Britain sunk in lucre's sordid charms,   145
And France revenged of ANNE's and EDWARD's arms!'
'Twas no Court-badge, great Scriv'ner, fired thy brain,
Nor lordly Luxury, nor City gain:
No, 'twas thy righteous end, ashamed to see
Senates degen'rate, Patriots disagree,   150
And, nobly wishing Party-rage to cease,
To buy both sides, and give thy Country peace.
    'All this is madness,' cries a sober sage:
But who, my friend, has reason in his rage?
'The ruling Passion, be it what it will,   155
The ruling Passion conquers Reason still.'
Less mad the wildest whimsey we can frame,
That even that Passion, if it has no Aim;
For though such motives Folly you may call,
The Folly's greater to have none at all.   160
    Hear then the truth: ' 'Tis Heaven each Passion sends,
And different men directs to different ends.
Extremes in Nature equal good produce,
Extremes in Man concur to general use.'
Ask we what makes one keep, and one bestow?   165
That POWER who bids the ocean ebb and flow,
Bids seed-time, harvest, equal course maintain,
Through reconciled extremes of drought and rain,

141 *Patriot* opposition member 142 *box* of the theatre, 143 *job* deal in shares
bite the town taste of high life 152 *buy both sides* the South Sea Company won
shareholders from both parties when it offered to take over the national debt.
155 *ruling passion* Pope expounds this theory in his *Essay on Man* II 123–44 and
To Cobham 174 ff. 167–8 see Genesis viii 22

Builds Life on Death, on Change Duration founds,
And gives the eternal wheels to know their rounds.   170
   Riches, like insects, when concealed they lie,
Wait but for wings, and in their season, fly.
Who sees pale Mammon pine amidst his store,
Sees but a backward steward for the Poor;
This year a Reservoir, to keep and spare;   175
The next, a Fountain, spouting through his Heir,
In lavish streams to quench a Country's thirst,
And men and dogs shall drink him till they burst.
   Old Cotta shamed his fortune and his birth,
Yet was not Cotta void of wit or worth: 180
What though (the use of barb'rous spits forgot)
His kitchen vied in coolness with his grot?
His court with nettles, moats with cresses stored,
With soups unbought and salads blessed his board?
If Cotta lived on pulse, it was no more   185
Than Brahmins, Saints, and Sages did before;
To cram the Rich was prodigal expense,
And who would take the Poor from Providence?
Like some lone Chartreux stands the good old Hall,
Silence without, and Fasts within the wall;   190
No raftered roofs with dance and tabor sound,
No noontide bell invites the country round:
Tenants with sighs the smokeless towers survey,
And turn th' unwilling steeds another way:
Benighted wanderers, the forest o'er,   195
Curse the saved candle, and unopening door;
While the gaunt mastiff growling at the gate,
Affrights the beggar whom he longs to eat.

171–2 see Proverbs xxiii 5; Pope has insects for the Bible's eagles; for analysis of this passage see headnote. *179 Cotta* Cutler* (?) *183–4* i.e. his weeds were his food. *189 Chartreux* Carthusian monastery *193 tenants* i.e. of the estate *194 unwilling steeds* plough-horses?

Not so his Son, he marked this oversight,
And then mistook reverse of wrong for right.　　　　200
(For what to shun will no great knowledge need,
But what to follow, is a task indeed.)
What slaughtered hecatombs, what floods of wine,
Fill the capacious Squire, and deep Divine!
Yet no mean motive this profusion draws,　　　　205
His oxen perish in his country's cause;
'Tis GEORGE and LIBERTY that crowns the cup,
And Zeal for that great House which eats him up.
The woods recede around the naked seat,
The Sylvans groan—no matter—for the Fleet:　　　　210
Next goes his Wool, to clothe our valiant bands;
Last, for his Country's love, he sells his Lands.
To town he comes, completes the nation's hope,
And heads the bold Train-bands, and burns a Pope.
And shall not Britain now reward his toils,　　　　215
Britain, that pays her Patriots with her Spoils?
In vain at Court the Bankrupt pleads his cause,
His thankless Country leaves him to her Laws.

　　The Sense to value Riches, with the Art
To enjoy them, and the Virtue to impart,　　　　220
Not meanly, nor ambitiously pursued,
Not sunk by sloth, not raised by servitude;
To balance Fortune by a just expense,
Join with Economy, Magnificence;
With Splendour, Charity; with Plenty, Health;　　　　225
Oh, teach us, BATHURST! yet unspoil'd by wealth!
That secret rare, between th' extremes to move
Of mad Good-nature, and of mean Self-love.
　　To Want or Worth well weighed, be Bounty given,
And ease, or emulate, the care of Heaven.　　　　230

203 hecatombs hundreds of sacrificial oxen *214 train-bands* companies of citizen soldiers; here led against the Catholic cause *224 magnificence* the liberality proper to the rich

Whose measure full o'erflows on human race,
Mend Fortune's fault, and justify her grace.
Wealth in the gross is death, but life diffused;
As Poison heals, in just proportion used:
In heaps, like Ambergris, a stink it lies,   235
But well-dispersed, is Incense to the Skies.

    Who starves by Nobles, or with Nobles eats?
The Wretch that trusts them, and the Rogue that cheats.
Is there a Lord, who knows a cheerful noon
Without a Fiddler, Flatt'rer, or Buffoon?   240
Whose table, Wit or modest Merit share,
Unelbow'd by a Gamester, Pimp, or Player?
Who copies Yours, or OXFORD's better part,
To ease th' oppressed, and raise the sinking heart?
Where'er he shines, oh Fortune, gild the scene,   245
And Angels guard him in the golden Men!
There, English bounty yet awhile may staand,
And Honour linger ere it leaves the land.

    But all our praises why should Lords engross?
Rise, honest Muse! and sing the MAN OF ROSS: 250
Pleased Vaga echoes through her winding bounds,
And rapid Severn hoarse applause resounds.
Who hung with woods yon mountain's sultry brow?
From the dry rock who bade the waters flow?
Not to the skies in useless columns tossed,   255
Or in proud falls magnificently lost,
But clear and artless, pouring through the plain
Health to the sick, and solace to the swain.
Whose Causeway parts the vale with shady rows?
Whose Seats the weary Traveller repose?   260
Who taught that heaven-directed spire to rise?

231-2 i.e. let the bountiful deserve their privilege by helping the unfortunate.
233 *gross* thick mass 235 *ambergris* whale's bowel-secretion, used to make scent
243 *Oxford* Harley* 250 *Man of Ross* Kyrle* 251 *Vaga* the Wye, a 'rambling'
river 254 Kyrle built a reservoir; and see Isaiah xlviii 21.

'The MAN OF ROSS,' each lisping babe replies.
Behold the Market-place with poor o'erspread!
The MAN OF ROSS divides the weekly bread:
He feeds yon Almshouse, neat, but void of state,   265
Where Age and Want sit smiling at the gate:
Him portioned maids, apprenticed orphans blest,
The young who labour, and the old who rest.
Is any sick? the MAN OF ROSS relieves,
Prescribes, attends, the medicine makes, and gives.   270
Is there a variance? enter but his door,
Balked are the courts, and contest is no more.
Despairing Quacks with curses fled the place,
And vile Attorneys, now an useless race.

   Thrice happy man! enabled to pursue   275
What all so wish, but want the power to do!
Oh say, what sums that gen'rous hand supply?
What mines, to swell that boundless charity?

   Of Debts and Taxes, Wife and Children clear,
This man possessed—five hundred pounds a year!   280
Blush, Grandeur, blush! proud Courts, withdraw your blaze!
Ye little Stars, hide your diminished rays.

   'And what? no monument, inscription, stone?
His race, his form, his name almost unknown?'
Who builds a Church to God, and not to Fame,   285
Will never mark the marble with his Name:
Go, search it there, where to be born, and die,
Of rich and poor makes all the history,
Enough that Virtue filled the space between;
Proved, by the ends of being, to have been.   290
When Hopkins dies, a thousand lights attend
The wretch, who living saved a candle's end;

---

279 Kyrle was a bachelor. *282 little stars* see *Paradise Lost* iv 34; perhaps with pun
on 'petty knights' *287* the Parish Register

Should'ring God's altar a vile image stands,
Belies his features, nay extends his hands;
That livelong wig which Gorgon's self might own,   295
Eternal buckle takes in Parian stone.
Behold what blessings Wealth to life can lend!
And see what comfort it affords our end.

   In the worst inn's worst room, with mat half-hung,
The floors of plaister, and the walls of dung,   300
On once a flock-bed, but repaired with straw,
With tape-tied curtains never meant to draw,
The George and Garter dangling from that bed
Where tawdry yellow strove with dirty red,
Great Villiers lies,—alas! how changed from him,   305
That life of pleasure, and that soul of whim!
Gallant and gay, in Cliveden's proud alcove,
The bower of wanton Shrewsbury and love;
Or just as gay, at Council, in a ring
Of mimicked statesmen, and their merry King.   310
No Wit to flatter, left of all his store!
No Fool to laugh at, which he valued more.
There, Victor of his health, of fortune, friends,
And fame; this lord of useless thousands ends.

   His Grace's fate sage Cutler could foresee,   315
And well (he thought) advised him, 'Live like me.'
As well his Grace replied, 'Like you, Sir John?
That I can do, when all I have is gone.'
Resolve me, Reason, which of these is worse,
Want with a full, or with an empty purse?   320

---

294 extends his hands Hopkins was 'tight-fisted' *295 livelong* everlasting *Gorgon*
serpent-haired monster that turned beholders to stone *296 Parian stone* a fine
marble *301 flock-bed* itself an inferior kind *305* echoes *Aeneid* ii 274, on the fallen
Hector; and see Introduction p. 18 *Villiers* Buckingham* *307 Cliveden* a great
house, once owned by Buckingham *308 Shrewsbury* Lady Shrewsbury, whose
husband was killed by her lover Buckingham in a duel she was supposed to have
attended as page.

Thy life more wretched, Cutler, was confessed,
Arise, and tell me, was thy death more blessed?
Cutler saw tenants break, and houses fall,
For very want; he could not build a wall.
His only daughter in a stranger's power,   325
For very want; he could not pay a dower.
A few grey hairs his rev'rend temples crowned;
'Twas very want that sold them for two pound.
What even denied a cordial at his end,
Banished the doctor, and expelled the friend?   330
What but a want, which you perhaps think mad,
Yet numbers feel, the want of what he had!
Cutler and Brutus, dying both exclaim,
'Virtue! and Wealth! what are ye but a name!'
    Say, for such worth are other worlds prepared?   335
Or are they both, in this their own reward?
A knotty point! to which we now proceed.
But you are tired—I'll tell a tale. 'Agreed.'
    Where London's column, pointing at the skies
Like a tall bully, lifts the head, and lies;   340
There dwelt a Citizen of sober fame,
A plain good man, and Balaam was his name;
Religious, punctual, frugal, and so forth;
His word would pass for more than he was worth.
One solid dish his week-day meal affords,   345
An added pudding solemnised the Lord's:
Constant at Church, and Change; his gains were sure,
His givings rare, save farthings to the poor.
    The Devil was piqued such saintship to behold,
And longed to tempt him, like good Job of old: 350

---

333 Brutus died exclaiming that virtue is an empty name *339–40* the Monument to the fire of London then bore an inscription blaming the fire on 'the Popish faction' *342 Balaam* the parable owes less to Balaam's story than to Job's, but Balaam was tempted with power, silver and gold; see Numbers xxii. *347 change* exchange

But Satan now is wiser than of yore,
And tempts by making rich, not making poor.

Roused by the Prince of Air, the whirlwinds sweep
The surge, and plunge his Father in the deep;
Then full against his Cornish lands they roar,   355
And two rich shipwrecks bless the lucky shore.

Sir Balaam now, he lives like other folks,
He takes his chirping pint, and cracks his jokes:
'Live like yourself,' was soon my Lady's word;
And lo! two puddings smoked upon the board.   360

Asleep and naked as an Indian lay,
An honest factor stole a Gem away:
He pledged it to the knight; the knight had wit,
So kept the Diamond, and the rogue was bit.
Some scruple rose, but thus he eased his thought,   365
'I'll now give sixpence where I gave a groat,
Where once I went to church, I'll now go twice—
And am so clear too of all other vice.'

The Tempter saw his time; the work he plied;
Stocks and Subscriptions pour on ev'ry side,   370
Till all the Dæmon makes his full descent
In one abundant shower of Cent. per Cent.;
Sinks deep within him, and possesses whole,
Then dubs Director, and secures his soul.

Behold Sir Balaam, now a man of spirit,   375
Ascribes his gettings to his parts and merit;
What late he called a Blessing, now was Wit,
And God's good Providence, a lucky Hit.
Things change their titles, as our manners turn:
His compting-house employed the Sunday morn: 380
Seldom at Church ('twas such a busy life),
But duly sent his family and wife.

---

356 lucky shore Pope refers in a note to the inhumanity of the Cornish people
when a wreck came their way *363 pledged* gave on promise of payment *366 groat*
fourpence

There (so the Devil ordained) one Christmastide
My good old Lady catched a cold, and died.

    A Nymph of Quality admires our Knight;   385
He marries, bows at Court, and grows polite:
Leaves the dull Cits, and joins (to please the fair)
The well-bred cuckolds in St James's air:
First, for his Son a gay Commission buys,
Who drinks, whores, fights, and in a duel dies: 390
His daughter flaunts a Viscount's tawdry-wife;
She bears a Coronet and Pox for life.
In Britain's Senate he a seat obtains,
And one more Pensioner St Stephen gains.
My Lady falls to play: so bad her chance,   395
He must repair it; takes a bribe from France;
The House impeach him; Coningsby harangues;
The Court forsake him—and Sir Balaam hangs.
Wife, son, and daughter, Satan, are thy own,
His wealth, yet dearer, forfeit to the Crown: 400
The Devil and the King divide the prize,
And sad Sir Balaam curses God, and dies.

*Epistle IV To Richard Boyle, Earl of Burlington: Of the Use of
    Riches (ii)*

This Epistle, which caused as much stir as any of Pope's poems,
was first published in 1731 with a title page declaring it to be for
the publication of 'Palladio's designs of the baths, arches, theatres,
etc., of ancient Rome' by Richard Boyle, Earl of Burlington. The
Burlington work referred to seems to be the one promised in a
1730 volume (which contains only the Roman bath designs) but
it was never issued. In 1730 Burlington addressed to his readers a
plea for good sense and temperance in building, and deplored the
current false taste for mere expense. Burlington helped Pope find

387 Cits dwellers in the city of London; 'mere tradesmen' *388 St James's* the
fashionable side of London *389 gay commission* i.e. in a fashionable regiment
394 St Stephen the Commons used to meet in St Stephen's Chapel.

both his Chiswick home, where he was a neighbour, and his Twickenham one (to which Pope moved in 1718). He favoured a certain reticence, economy and cleanliness of line in architecture, with conformity to a human scale.

The first intention of the poem, it seems, was to offer an essay on prodigality. The theme remains but is surpassed and subsumed under the larger theme of 'bounty'. The profusion of money and the profusion of nature must alike be properly regulated and cultivated; it is thus that the arts of architecture and gardening meet, and both are nourished on good sense:

> 'Tis use alone that sanctifies expense,
> And splendour borrows all her rays from sense.

It is perhaps no accident that the name of the 'oligarch' (as Empsom calls him) is Timon. For Shakespeare's *Timon of Athens* ranges over the same variety of attitudes to money as do the third and fourth Epistles.

With a superb confidence of address Pope represents gardening as at its best an heroic activity:

> Behold Villario's ten years' toil complete;
> His quincunx darkens, his espaliers meet;   80
> The wood supports the plain, the parts unite,
> And strength of shade contends with strength of light.

The principles affirmed here are consonant with those of William Kent—landscape gardener, architect and friend to Burlington—and perfectly accord with Pope's own practice, for in his own five acres at Twickenham he had his espaliers and a thicket composed of quincunxes. They are the principles flaunted too in the line, 'Spontaneous beauties all around advance', with its two senses of 'advance'. But they fail for long to sustain 'Villario':

> Tired of the scenes parterres and fountains yield,
> He finds at last he better likes a field.

Villario, if we may trust 'A Master Key to Popery' which has reached us in MS and may even be Pope's own work, was a Chiswick neighbour who was in the habit of taking walks in the fields, getting away from his finely planned garden. The observation that Pope makes upon him seems to be a wry one, for this is just where the cult of nature as opposed to artifice might lead. The lines are apt to be remembered when we reach the more richly suggestive ones at 173–6.

The outcry about the poem centred on the alleged attack mounted on the Duke of Chandos under cover of Timon. Pope denied any connection and Chandos himself magnanimously accepted the denials. Contemporaries might be excused, however, for supposing that any allusion to vast and pretentious building would include a glance at Canons, which Pope knew well and where he was often a guest. Hogarth was one of the many who refused to take the disclaimers seriously. In a famous print he represented Pope whitewashing Burlington Gate in Piccadilly, with some of the wash splashing a figure standing near a coach which bears ducal crests at three corners and a crescent on the fourth; one of the captions reads: 'not a Dukes coach as appears by the crescent at one Corner'.

Critical discussion of this poem is to be found in F. W. Bateson's Twickenham edition, in F. R. Leavis's *Revaluations*, W. Empsom's *Seven Types of Ambiguity* and R. A. Brower's *Pope: the Poetry of Allusion*.

For the gardening and architecture see Margaret Jourdain, *The Work of William Kent* (1948), James Lees-Milne, *Earls of Creation* (*1962*) and M. L. Gothein, *A History of Garden Art*, Vol. II. Surviving examples of Burlington's Palladian style include Chiswick Villa and the York Assembly Rooms. Among Vanbrugh's works are Castle Howard in the North Riding, and Blenheim Palace—a 'laboured quarry' on a more than human scale. For the poem's satirical use of scale compare the Brobdignag chapters of *Gulliver's Travels* and Fielding's farce *Tom Thumb*.

In the first editions the Timon passage had come just before the closing address to Burlington, which then included the present lines 23–38. Lines 169–76, which first preceded Timon, now follow as a mollifying postscript.

The typography is basically that of 1744.

EPISTLE IV

TO RICHARD BOYLE, EARL OF BURLINGTON

OF THE USE OF RICHES

'TIS strange, the Miser should his Cares employ,
To gain those Riches he can ne'er enjoy:
Is it less strange, the Prodigal should waste
His wealth, to purchase what he ne'er can taste?
Not for himself he sees, or hears, or eats;   5
Artists must choose his Pictures, Music, Meats:
He buys for Topham, Drawings and Designs,
For Pembroke Statues, dirty Gods, and Coins;
Rare monkish Manuscripts for Hearne alone,
And books for Mead, and butterflies for Sloane.   10
Think we all these are for himself? no more
Than his fine Wife, alas! or finer whore.
     For what has Virro painted, built, and planted?
Only to show, how many tastes he wanted.
What brought Sir Visto's ill-got wealth to waste?   15
Some Dæmon whispered, 'Visto! have a Taste.'
Heaven visits with a Taste the wealthy fool,
And needs no Rod but Ripley with a Rule.

7–10 the names are of distinguished collectors. 13 Virro from 'virus'? 15 Visto meaning 'prospect', 'vista' 18 rod i.e. measure of taste Ripley Pope calls him a carpenter raised to architect by a prime minister.

See! sportive fate, to punish awkward pride,
Bids Bubo build, and sends him such a Guide: 20
A standing sermon, at each year's expense,
That never Coxcomb reached Magnificence!
 You show us, Rome was glorious, not profuse,
And pompous buildings once were things of Use.
Yet shall (my Lord) your just, your noble rules   25
Fill half the land with Imitating Fools;
Who random drawings from your sheets shall take,
And of one beauty many blunders make;
Load some vain Church with old Theatric state,
Turn Arcs of triumph to a Garden-gate;   30
Reverse your Ornaments, and hang them all
On some patched dog-hole eked with ends of wall;
Then clap four slices of Pilaster on 't,
That, laced with bits of rustic, makes a Front.
Or call the winds through long Arcades to roar,   35
Proud to catch cold at a Venetian door;
Conscious they act a true Palladian part,
And, if they starve, they starve by rules of art.
 Oft have you hinted to your brother Peer
A certain truth, which many buy too dear: 40
Something there is more needful than Expense,
And something previous even to Taste—'tis Sense:
Good Sense, which only is the gift of Heaven,
And though no science, fairly worth the seven:
A Light, which in yourself you must perceive;   45
Jones and Le Nôtre have it not to give.

---

20 Bubo (meaning 'owl') Dodington*; his 'guide' was Vanbrugh.* *30* Lord
Peterborough's* gate resembled a triumphal arch; see Ep. ii 289 *34 rustic* rough
masonry *36 Venetian door* i.e. in the style favoured by Palladio, the Venetian
architect *39 brother Peer* i.e. one like Bubo, who confuses expense with magnificence *44 the seven* i.e. grammar, logic, rhetoric (the Trivium); arithmetic,
music, geometry, astronomy (the Quadrivium) *46 Jones* Inigo Jones the
celebrated architect *Le Nôtre* the gardener responsible for the symmetrical style
of Versailles

To build, to plant, whatever you intend,
To rear the Column, or the Arch to bend,
To swell the Terrace, or to sink the Grot;
In all, let Nature never be forgot.   50
But treat the goddess like a modest fair,
Nor over-dress, nor leave her wholly bare;
Let not each beauty everywhere be spied,
Where half the skill is decently to hide.
He gains all points, who pleasingly confounds,   55
Surprises, varies, and conceals the Bounds.
   Consult the Genius of the Place in all:
That tells the Waters or to rise, or fall;
Or helps the ambitious Hill the heaven to scale,
Or scoops in circling theatres the Vale;   60
Calls in the Country, catches opening glades,
Joins willing woods, and varies shades from shades,
Now breaks, or now directs, the intending Lines;
Paints as you plant, and, as you work, designs.
   Still follow Sense, of every Art the Soul,   65
Parts answering parts shall slide into a whole,
Spontaneous beauties all around advance,
Start ev'n from Difficulty, strike from Chance;
Nature shall join you, Time shall make it grow
A Work to wonder at—perhaps a Stowe.   70
   Without it, proud Versailles! thy glory falls;
And Nero's Terraces desert their walls:
The vast Parterres a thousand hands shall make,
Lo! Cobham comes, and floats them with a Lake:
Or cut wide views through Mountains to the Plain,   75
You'll wish your hill or sheltered seat again.

---

60 circling theatres rounded views, with hint of amphitheatre terraces *63 intending* eye-directing *70 Stowe* Cobham's* house and garden *72 Nero* his palace gardens were on a mountainside *73 parterres* level flowerbeds *hands* i.e. gardeners *74 floats* floods *75* this was done in Hertfordshire by the financier Benjamin Styles. *76 wish* i.e. wish for *seat* i.e. residence

Even in an ornament its place remark,
Nor in an Hermitage set Dr Clarke.
Behold Villario's ten years' toil complete;
His Quincunx darkens, his Espaliers meet;   80
The Wood supports the Plain, the parts unite,
And strength of Shade contends with strength of Light;
A waving Glow his bloomy beds display,
Blushing in bright diversities of day,
With silver-quivering rills meandered o'er—   85
Enjoy them, you! Villario can no more:
Tired of the scene Parterres and Fountains yield,
He finds at last he better likes a Field.

Through his young Woods how pleased Sabinus strayed,
Or sat delighted in the thick'ning shade,   90
With annual joy the redd'ning shoots to greet,
Or see the stretching branches long to meet!
His Son's fine Taste an opener Vista loves,
Foe to the Dryads of his Father's groves;
One boundless Green, or flourished Carpet views,   95
With all the mournful family of Yews:
The thriving plants, ignoble broomsticks made,
Now sweep those Alleys they were born to shade.

At Timon's Villa let us pass a day,
Where all cry out, 'What sums are thrown away!'   100
So proud, so grand, of that stupendous air,
Soft and Agreeable come never there.
Greatness, with Timon, dwells in such a draught
As brings all Brobdignag before your thought.
To compass this, his building is a Town,   105
His pond an Ocean, his parterre a Down:

*78 Dr Clarke** a highly sociable Divine; his bust was set with others in the Queen's Hermitage or garden retreat *80 quincunx* group of five trees, with four at the corners and one at the centre *espalier* lattice-trained tree *86 Villario* type-name from 'villa' *89 Sabinus* from a common Roman name *95 flourished* flowered *99 Timon* after the prodigal Greek in Plutarch's 'Lives'; with a glance at Chandos** *101 of that* of such *103 draught* design; with a pun?

Who but must laugh, the Master when he sees,
A puny insect, shivering at a breeze!
Lo, what huge heaps of littleness around!
The whole, a laboured Quarry above ground,   110
Two Cupids squirt before: a Lake behind
Improves the keenness of the Northern wind.
His Gardens next your admiration call,
On every side you look, behold the Wall!
No pleasing Intricacies intervene,   115
No artful wildness to perplex the scene:
Grove nods at grove, each Alley has a brother,
And half the platform just reflects the other.
The suff'ring eye inverted Nature sees,
Trees cut to Statues, Statues thick as trees;   120
With here a Fountain, never to be played;
And there a Summer-house, that knows no shade:
Here Amphitrite sails through myrtle bowers;
There Gladiators fight, or die, in flowers;
Unwatered see the drooping sea-horse mourn,   125
And swallows roost in Nilus' dusty Urn.

My Lord advances with majestic mien,
Smit with the mighty pleasure, to be seen:
But soft—by regular approach—not yet—
First through the length of yon hot Terrace sweat;   130
And when up ten steep slopes you've dragged your thighs,
Just at his Study-door he'll bless your eyes.

His Study! with what Authors is it stored?
In Books, not Authors, curious is my Lord;
To all their dated Backs he turns you round;   135
These Aldus printed, those Du Suëil has bound.

---

110 laboured quarry mass of stonework; with a glance at Blenheim *122* fountains too ambitious for the water-supply. *123 Amphitrite* wife of Poseidon, the water-god *124* Pope refers in a note to the famous Roman statues of the fighting and dying gladiators. *136 Aldus* early Venetian printer *Du Suëil* a Parisian book-binder

Lo, some are Vellum, and the rest as good
For all his Lordship knows, but they are Wood.
For Locke or Milton 'tis in vain to look,
These shelves admit not any modern book.   140
    And now the Chapel's silver bell you hear,
That summons you to all the Pride of Prayer:
Light quirks of Music, broken and uneven,
Make the soul dance upon a Jig to Heaven.
On painted Ceilings you devoutly stare,   145
Where sprawl the Saints of Verrio or Laguerre,
Or gilded clouds in fair expansion lie,
And bring all Paradise before your eye.
To rest, the Cushion and soft Dean invite,
Who never mentions Hell to ears polite.   150
    But hark! the chiming Clocks to dinner call;
A hundred footsteps scrape the marble Hall:
The rich Buffet well-coloured Serpents grace,
And gaping Tritons spew to wash your face.
Is this a dinner? this a Genial room?   155
No, 'tis a Temple, and a Hecatomb.
A solemn Sacrifice, perform'd in state,
You drink by measure, and to minutes eat.
So quick retires each flying course, you'd swear
Sancho's dread Doctor and his Wand were there.   160
Between each Act the trembling salvers ring,
From soup to sweet-wine, and God bless the King.
In plenty starving, tantalized in state,
And complaisantly helped to all I hate,
Treated, caressed, and tired, I take my leave,   165
Sick of his civil Pride from Morn to Eve;

146 Verrio painted ceilings at Windsor and Hampton Court *Laguerre* painted ceilings at Blenheim *148 Paradise* notice the innuendo *149 Dean* Chetwood, who found it not decent to name the place of punishment before the 'polite' Court *153 buffet* sideboard; here of carved and painted wood *156 hecatomb* a sacrifice of a hundred oxen *160 Sancho* see *Don Quixote* xlvii

I curse such lavish cost, and little skill,
And swear no Day was ever passed so ill.

    Yet hence the Poor are clothed, the Hungry fed;
Health to himself, and to his Infants bread,   170
The Lab'rer bears: what his hard Heart denies,
His charitable Vanity supplies.

    Another age shall see the golden Ear
Imbrown the Slope, and nod on the Parterre,
Deep Harvests bury all his pride has planned,   175
And laughing Ceres reassume the land.

    Who then shall grace, or who improve the Soil?—
Who plants like Bathurst, or who builds like Boyle.
'Tis Use alone that sanctifies Expense,
And Splendour borrows all her rays from Sense.   180

    His Father's Acres who enjoys in peace,
Or makes his Neighbours glad, if he increase:
Whose cheerful Tenants bless their yearly toil,
Yet to their Lord owe more than to the soil;
Whose ample Lawns are not ashamed to feed   185
The milky heifer and deserving steed;
Whose rising Forests, not for pride or show,
But future Buildings, future Navies grow:
Let his plantations stretch from down to down,
First shade a Country, and then raise a Town.   190

    You too proceed! make falling Arts your care,
Erect new wonders, and the old repair;
Jones and Palladio to themselves restore,
And be whate'er Vitruvius was before:

171–6 refer to the demolition of extravagantly built houses; Canons, home of
Chandos,* was pulled down three years after Pope's death. *176 Ceres* goddess
representing the fruitfulness of nature *185 lawns* meadows, with hint of modern
meaning *190 raise* foster, feed *194 Vitruvius* architectural writer influential in
Caesar's Rome *194–205* Pope says in a note that many English roads were im-
passable, several newly built London churches were ready to fall, the bridge
scheme for Westminster had been rejected, and much flood damage had been done
through an embankment breach at Dagenham.

'Till Kings call forth the Ideas of your mind,   195
Proud to accomplish what such hands design'd,
Bid Harbours open, public Ways extend,
Bid Temples, worthier of the God, ascend;
Bid the broad Arch the dang'rous Flood contain,
The Mole projected break the roaring Main;   200
Back to his bounds their subject Sea command,
And roll obedient Rivers through the Land;
These Honours Peace to happy Britain brings,
These are Imperial Works, and worthy Kings.

200 *mole* pier or causeway

Satires and Imitations of Horace

Epistle to Arbuthnot: Prologue to the Satires

WRITING from his death-bed in 1734 Arbuthnot, friend, physician and fellow-wit, pleaded with Pope to continue his 'noble disdain and abhorrence of vice' but to study 'more to reform than chastise', however difficult it may be to do one without the other. Pope answered that general satire lacked force and some individuals had therefore to be held up as examples, and Arbuthnot responded with a warning that in risking ill-will Pope was endangering his own safety. The situation, in fact, resembled the fictional situation (friend warning satirist) of *To Fortescue*, the imitation of Horace's 1st Satire of Book II, which Pope had published in 1733. Finding occasion ripe, Pope offered to address to Arbuthnot an Epistle, 'written by piecemeal many years, and which I have now made haste to put together; wherein the question is stated, what were and are my motives of writing, the objections to them and my answers'.

The Epistle is therefore both a literary exercise in the Horatian manner and, in so far as it sprang out of Arbuthnot's concern for Pope and Pope's for Arbuthnot, a highly personal *apologia* enlisting intimacies of feeling hardly appropriate to the Horatian form. It is more than a defence of the satirist; it is also a plea for the ego. We are made more than usually conscious of the vulnerable man behind the cultivated mask:

> The Muse but served to ease some friend, not wife,
> To help me through this long disease, my life.

Pope suffered from a deformity of the spine, from asthma, an eye-disease and (at the end) from dropsy. This sufficiently explains the touches of self-dramatization and self-pity that make the *Prologue* one of the most 'human' and therefore popular of the poems.

Nevertheless, the Epistle has its impersonal quality too, and it is a pity that this has sometimes been forgotten and the Atticus and Sporus characters been too promptly referred to Pope's personal motives for creating them. Each, like the apparently anonymous Codrus passage, owes its success to insights that have nothing to do with malice. Atticus is made a fully representative figure whose fine urbanity is subtly contaminated by overbred arrogance; his faults are of a piece with the civilization to which he belongs. Sporus, like Codrus (see Introduction, p. 21), exemplifies creation gone wrong; as if in mimicry of his own wit he is 'one vile antithesis' and he corrupts society as the serpent (whose presence is felt in the verse) corrupted Eve:

Wit that can creep, and pride that licks the dust.

Nero's minion lives still, an exemplary parasite, and again the kind of creature that is spawned in an over-sophisticated society.

That Atticus was Addison (who, it is said, taught critics to sneer at Pope's Homer) and Sporus Lord Hervey does not spoil the representativeness of the figures in the poem; it might indeed be argued that both were highly representative in fact, as well as in these fictions. This is not to say that Pope's portraits are objective and just. Their art is in the extravagance, the caricature, the mythologizing which is brought to its highest point in *The Dunciad*—that joyous but frightening indictment of a whole civilization. But is it a 'whole civilization', or is it merely a Whig aspect of it seen through jaded Tory eyes? The Satires, from their Prologue to their Epilogue, supply ample material for several kinds of answer to this unsettling question.

Following the Twickenham editor's decision I have dropped

the dialogue form apparently introduced by, or on the advice of, Pope's first editor Warburton. In the dialogue version, 'A.' (Arbuthnot) is credited with interventions at 74–8, 101–4, 305–8, 361, 390 and 418–19. The typography is basically that of 1734.

"... I hope to deter, if not to reform

EPISTLE TO ARBUTHNOT

PROLOGUE TO THE SATIRES

SHUT, shut the door, good *John*! fatigued, I said;
Tie up the knocker, say I'm sick, I'm dead.
The Dog-star rages! nay 'tis past a doubt,
All *Bedlam*, or *Parnassus*, is let out:
Fire in each eye, and Papers in each hand, 5
They rave, recite, and madden round the land.

What Walls can guard me, or what Shades can hide?
They pierce my Thickets, through my Grot they glide,
By land, by water, they renew the charge,
They stop the Chariot, and they board the Barge. 10
No place is sacred, not the Church is free,
Ev'n *Sunday* shines no *Sabbath-day* to me:
Then from the *Mint* walks forth the Man of Rhyme,
Happy! to catch me, just at Dinner-time.

Mrs. Barber Is there a Parson, much bemused in Beer, *Rev. Laurence Eusden* 15
A maudlin Poetess, a rhyming Peer,
A Clerk, foredoom'd his Father's soul to cross,
Who pens a Stanza, when he should *engross*?
Is there, who, locked from Ink and Paper, scrawls
With desperate Charcoal round his darkened walls? 20

1 John Serle, Pope's servant *3 dog-star* Sirius in the Greater Dog, associated with August heat and the season of roman poetry-rehearsals *8 grot* grotto at Twickenham *10 barge* used by Pope between Twickenham and London *12 Sabbath* day of rest *13 Mint* used as debtors' sanctuary *15 Parson* Eusden, a minor poet; name concealed in 'be-mus'd in' *17 soul to cross* will to thwart *18 engross* write legal hand *20 darkened walls* of the madhouse

"But General Satire in Times of General Vice has no force, & is no Punishment. ... 'tis only by hunting One or Two from the other...

All fly to *Twit'nam*, and in humble strain
Apply to me, to keep them mad or vain.
Arthur, whose giddy Son neglects the Laws,
Imputes to me and my damned works the cause:
Poor *Cornus* sees his frantic Wife elope,   25
And curses Wit, and Poetry, and *Pope*.

    Friend to my life! (which did not you prolong,
The World had wanted many an idle Song)
What *Drop* or *Nostrum* can this Plague remove?
Or which must end me, a Fool's Wrath or Love?   30
A dire Dilemma! either way I'm sped.
If Foes, they write, if Friends, they read me dead.
Seized and tied down to judge, how wretched I!
Who can't be silent, and who will not lie:
To laugh, were want of Goodness and of Grace,   35
And to be grave, exceeds all Power of Face.
I sit with sad Civility, I read
With honest anguish, and an aching head;
And drop at last, but in unwilling ears,
This saving counsel,—'Keep your Piece nine years.'   40

    'Nine years!' cries he, who, high in *Drury Lane*,
Lulled by soft Zephyrs through the broken Pane,
Rhymes ere he wakes, and prints before *Term* ends,
Obliged by hunger, and Request of friends:
'The Piece, you think, is incorrect: why take it,   45
I'm all submission, what you'd have it, make it.'

    Three things another's modest wishes bound,
My Friendship, and a Prologue, and ten Pound.
Pitholeon sends to me: 'You know his Grace,
I want a Patron; ask him for a Place.'   50

23 *Arthur* Moore, a poet's son and the 'clerk' of l. 17 25 *Cornus* any cuckold 29 *drop, nostrum* quack remedies 31 *sped* done for 33 *tied down to judge* this happens in Wycherley's *Plain Dealer* v. 3 40 *piece* a pun? 41 *Drury Lane* then a disreputable street 43 *Term* legal term and publishing season 44 *request of friends* common excuse in prefaces 49 *Pitholeon* foolish poet named in Horace; applied to Welsted*

Pitholeon libelled me—'But here's a Letter
Informs you Sir, 'twas when he knew no better.
Dare you refuse him? *Curll* invites to dine,
He'll write a *Journal*, or he'll turn *Divine*.'
    Bless me! a Packet. ' 'Tis a stranger sues,   55
A Virgin Tragedy, an Orphan Muse.'
If I dislike it, 'Furies, death and rage!'
If I approve, 'Commend it to the Stage.'
There (thank my Stars) my whole Commission ends,
The Players and I are, luckily, no friends.   60
Fired that the House reject him, ' 'Sdeath! I'll print it,
And shame the Fools—your Interest, Sir, with *Lintot*.'
Lintot, dull rogue! will think your price too much:
'Not, Sir, if you revise it, and retouch.'
All my demurs but double his attacks: 65
And last he whispers, 'Do, and we go snacks.'
Glad of a quarrel, straight I clap the door:
Sir, let me see your works and you no more.
    'Tis sung, when *Midas*' Ears began to spring
(*Midas*, a sacred Person and a King),   70
His very Minister who spied them first
(Some say his Queen) was forced to speak, or burst:
And is not mine, my Friend, a sorer case,
When every Coxcomb perks them in my face?
    'Good friend, forbear! you deal in dang'rous things,   75
I'd never name Queens, Ministers, or Kings:
Keep close to Ears, and those let Asses prick,
'Tis nothing—' Nothing? if they bite and kick?
Out with it, *Dunciad*! let the secret pass,
That Secret to each Fool, that he's an Ass: 80

54 i.e. to attack Pope publicly in print and sermon *61 house* playhouse *66 go
snacks* share profits *72* Ovid says Midas's barber spied his ass's ears; Chaucer's
Wife of Bath says the Queen *76* glances at Walpole's alliance with the Queen
80 ass i.e. a manifest fool

126

for his own conscience sake — & peace of mind

The truth once told (and wherefore should we lie?)
The Queen of *Midas* slept, and so may I.
  You think this cruel? Take it for a rule,
No creature smarts so little as a Fool.
Let Peals of Laughter, *Codrus*! round thee break,   85
Thou unconcern'd canst hear the mighty Crack:
Pit, Box, and Gallery in convulsions hurl'd,
Thou stand'st unshook amidst a bursting World. *lack of shame*
Who shames a Scribbler? break one cobweb through,
He spins the slight, self-pleasing thread anew: 90
Destroy his Fib or Sophistry; in vain,
The Creature's at his dirty work again;
Thron'd in the Centre of his thin designs,
Proud of a vast Extent of flimsy lines!
Whom have I hurt? has Poet yet, or Peer,   95
Lost the arch'd eyebrow, or *Parnassian* sneer?   *Colley Cibber*
And has not *Colley* still his lord, and whore?   *John*
His butchers *Henley*, his Freemasons *Moore*?   *Lady Mary Wortley Montagu*
Does not one table *Bavius* still admit?
Still to one bishop *Philips* seem a wit?   100
Still *Sappho*—'Hold! for God's sake—you'll offend: *he has*
No Names—be calm—learn Prudence of a Friend.
I too could write, and I am twice as tall;   *not worrin bothering about*
But Foes like these—' One flatterer's worse than all.   (not Pope's level)
Of all mad Creatures, if the Learn'd are right,   105
It is the Slaver kills, and not the Bite.
A Fool quite angry is quite innocent:
Alas! 'tis ten times worse when they *repent*.
  One dedicates in high Heroic prose,
And ridicules beyond a hundred foes: 110

a petty poet

85 Codrus Roman poetaster; here a playwright *91 fib* lie, with hint of 'fibre' *93–4
designs . . . lines* punning on the 'plots' and 'lines' of a play *97 Colly* Cibber* *98
Henley** once addressed a sermon to butchers *Moore* J. M. Smythe* *99 Bavius*
Roman poetaster scorned by Virgil *101 Sappho* Lady Montagu* *106 slaver* saliva
(of a mad dog)

One from all *Grub Street* will my fame defend,
And, more abusive, calls himself my friend.
This prints my Letters, that expects a Bribe,
And others roar aloud, 'Subscribe, subscribe!'

There are, who to my Person pay their court: 115
I cough like *Horace*, and, though lean, am short.
Ammon's great son one shoulder had too high—
Such *Ovid*'s nose,—and, 'Sir! you have an *Eye*.'
Go on, obliging Creatures, make me see
All that disgraced my Betters, met in me.   120
Say for my comfort, languishing in bed,
'Just so immortal *Maro* held his head';
And when I die, be sure you let me know
Great *Homer* died three thousand years ago.

Why did I write? what sin to me unknown   125
Dipped me in Ink, my Parents', or my own?
As yet a Child, nor yet a Fool to Fame,
I lisped in Numbers, for the Numbers came.
I left no Calling for this idle trade,
No Duty broke, no Father disobey'd: 130
The Muse but served to ease some Friend, not Wife,
To help me through this long Disease, my Life;
To second, ARBUTHNOT! thy Art and Care,
And teach the Being you preserved, to bear.

But why then publish? *Granville* the polite,   135
And knowing *Walsh*, would tell me I could write;
Well-natured *Garth* inflamed with early praise,
And *Congreve* loved, and *Swift* endured my Lays;
The Courtly Talbot, Somers, Sheffield read,
Even mitred *Rochester* would nod the head,   140
And *St John*'s self (great *Dryden*'s friends before)

113 *this prints* i.e. Curll* 114 *subscribe* to the purchase of a book 116 *lean . . .
short* Horace was fat and short 117 i.e. Alexander the Great 122 *Maro* Virgil
129–30 see 17–23 137 *inflamed* encouraged 140 *Rochester* Atterbury* 141 *St John*
Bolingbroke* 141 *Dryden's friends* referring to the ten just named

With open arms received one Poet more.
Happy my Studies, when by these approved!
Happier their Author, when by these belov'd!
From these the world will judge of Men and Books,   145
Not from the *Burnets*, *Oldmixons*, and *Cookes*.
  Soft were my Numbers; who could take offence
While pure Description held the place of Sense?
Like gentle *Fanny's* was my flowery Theme,
A painted Mistress, or a purling Stream.   150
Yet then did *Gildon* draw his venal quill;
I wish'd the man a dinner, and sate still.
Yet then did *Dennis* rave in furious fret;
I never answered—I was not in debt:
If want provoked, or madness made them print,   155
I waged no war with *Bedlam* or the *Mint*.
  Did some more sober Critic come abroad?
If wrong, I smiled; if right, I kissed the rod.
Pains, reading, study, are their just pretence,
And all they want is spirit, taste, and sense.   160
Commas and points they set exactly right,
And 'twere a sin to rob them of their Mite;
Yet ne'er one sprig of Laurel graced these ribalds,
From slashing *Bentley* down to piddling *Tibbalds*:
Each Wight, who reads not, and but scans and spells,   165
Each Word-catcher, that lives on syllables,
Even such small Critics, some regard may claim,
Preserved in *Milton's* or in *Shakespeare's* name.
Pretty! in Amber to observe the forms
Of hairs, or straws, or dirt, or grubs, or worms;   170
The things, we know, are neither rich nor rare,
But wonder how the Devil they got there,
  Were others angry? I excused them too;
Well might they rage, I gave them but their due.

149 Fanny Hervey* *164 Bentley* as editor of *Paradise Lost* *piddling* trifling
Tibbald Theobald* as Shakespeare editor

E   129

A man's true merit 'tis not hard to find; 175
But each man's secret standard in his mind,
That Casting-weight Pride adds to Emptiness,
This, who can gratify, for who can *guess*?
The Bard whom pilfered Pastorals renown,
Who turns a *Persian* tale for half-a-crown, 180
Just writes to make his barrenness appear,
And strains from hard-bound brains, eight lines a-year;
He, who still wanting though he lives on theft,
Steals much, spends little, yet has nothing left:
And he, who now to sense, now nonsense leaning, 185
Means not, but blunders round about a meaning:
And he, whose Fustian's so sublimely bad,
It is not Poetry, but Prose run mad:
All these, my modest Satire bade *translate*,
And own'd that nine such Poets made a Tate. 190
How did they fume, and stamp, and roar, and chafe!
And swear, not *Addison* himself was safe.

Peace to all such! but were there One whose fires
True Genius kindles, and fair Fame inspires:
Blest with each Talent, and each Art to please, 195
And born to write, converse, and live with ease;
Should such a man, too fond to rule alone,
Bear, like the *Turk*, no brother near the throne,
View him with scornful, yet with jealous eyes,
And hate for Arts that caused himself to rise; 200
Damn with faint praise, assent with civil leer,
And without sneering, teach the rest to sneer;
Willing to wound, and yet afraid to strike,
Just hint a fault, and hesitate dislike;

176–8 i.e. 'who can satisfy a vain man's estimate of his own worth?' *standard* i.e. standard weight *179 bard* Philips* *renown* make famous *182 hard-bound* costive *189 bade translate* made a bid to transform *190* an ambiguous compliment to Nahum Tate* *197 fond* infatuated *198* Turkish rulers had this reputation *200 arts* the writer's skills and the politician's machinations

Alike reserved to blame, or to commend,   205
A tim'rous foe, and a suspicious friend;
Dreading even fools, by Flatterers besieged,
And so obliging, that he ne'er obliged;
Like *Cato*, give his little Senate laws,
And sit attentive to his own applause;   210
While Wits and Templars every sentence raise,
And wonder with a foolish face of praise.
Who but must laugh, if such a man there be?
Who would not weep, if *Atticus* were he?

    What though my Name stood rubric on the walls,   215
Or plastered posts, with Claps, in capitals?
Or smoking forth, a hundred Hawkers load,
On Wings of Winds came flying all abroad?
I sought no homage from the Race that write;
I kept, like *Asian* monarchs, from their sight: 220
Poems I heeded (now be-rhymed so long)
No more than Thou, great George! a Birthday Song.
I ne'er with Wits or Witlings passed my days,
To spread about the Itch of Verse and Praise;
Nor like a Puppy, daggled through the Town,   225
To fetch and carry, Sing-song up and down;
Nor at Rehearsals sweat, and mouthed, and cried,
With Handkerchief and Orange at my side;
But sick of Fops, and Poetry, and Prate,
To *Bufo* left the whole *Castalian* state.   230
    Proud as *Apollo* on his forked hill,
Sate full-blown *Bufo*, puffed by every quill;

---

208 i.e. 'so concerned with being polite that he never rendered a service' 209 *Cato*
hero of Addison's tragedy, to which Pope wrote a prologue including a version
of this line 214 *Atticus* Addison* 215 *rubric* red letters, in Lintot's* shop 216
claps posters 218 from a version of Psalm xviii 10 225 *daggled* trailed through
mud 227 *sweat* = sweated 230 *Bufo* (meaning 'a toad') any patron, with glances
at Halifax* and Dodington* *Castalian* of the muses (from a spring on Parnassus)
232 *puffed* puns on 'advertised'

Fed with soft Dedication all day long,
Horace and he went hand in hand in song.
His library (where Busts of Poets dead   235
And a true *Pindar* stood without a head)
Received of Wits an undistinguished race,
Who first his Judgment asked, and then a Place:
Much they extolled his Pictures, much his Seat,
And flattered ev'ry day, and some days eat: 240
Till grown more frugal in his riper days,
He paid some Bards with Port, and some with Praise,
To some a dry Rehearsal was assigned,
And others (harder still) he paid in kind.
Dryden alone (what wonder?) came not nigh,   245
Dryden alone escaped this judging eye:
But still the Great have kindness in reserve,
He help'd to bury whom he helped to starve.
    May some choice Patron bless each grey goose quill!
May every *Bavius* have his *Bufo* still!   250
So when a Statesman wants a Day's defence,
Or Envy holds a whole Week's war with Sense,
Or simple Pride for Flatt'ry makes demands,
May Dunce by Dunce be whistled off my hands!
Bless'd be the *Great*! for those they take away,   255
And those they left me—for they left me GAY;
Left me to see neglected Genius bloom,
Neglected die, and tell it on his Tomb:
Of all thy blameless Life the sole Return
My verse, and QUEENSBERRY weeping o'er thy Urn!   260
Oh let me live my own, and die so too!
('To live and die is all I have to do:')

---

235 a joke against antiquaries *240 eat* = ate *243 dry rehearsal* i.e. recital without
port *244 in kind* with his own verse (?) or with praise (?) *248* Dryden was given
a magnificent funeral. *251 day's defence* vindication in a journal *254 whistled off* a
falconry term *260 Queensberry* Charles Douglas* *262* quoted from Denham, *Of
Prudence*, line 94

Maintain a Poet's Dignity and Ease,
And see what friends, and read what books I please.
Above a Patron, though I condescend   265
Sometimes to call a Minister my Friend.
I was not born for Courts or great Affairs:
I pay my Debts, believe, and say my Prayers;
Can sleep without a Poem in my head,
Nor know if *Dennis* be alive or dead.   270

Why am I asked, 'what next shall see the light?'
Heavens! was I born for nothing but to write?
Has Life no Joys for me? or (to be grave)
Have I no Friend to serve, no Soul to save?
'I found him close with *Swift*'—'Indeed? no doubt,'   275
(Cries prating *Balbus*) 'something will come out.'
'Tis all in vain, deny it as I will:
'No, such a Genius never can lie still';
And then for mine obligingly mistakes
The first lampoon Sir *Will* or *Bubo* makes.   280
Poor guiltless I! and can I choose but smile,
When every Coxcomb knows me by my *Style*?

Cursed be the Verse, how well soe'er it flow,
That tends to make one worthy Man my foe,
Give Virtue scandal, Innocence a fear,   285
Or from the soft-eyed Virgin steal a tear!
But he, who hurts a harmless neighbour's peace,
Insults fall'n Worth, or Beauty in distress,
Who loves a Lie, lame slander helps about,
Who writes a Libel, or who copies out;   290
That Fop, whose pride affects a Patron's name,
Yet absent, wounds an Author's honest fame;
Who can your Merit selfishly approve,
And show the Sense of it without the Love;

276 Balbus Lord Dupplin, an incessant talker *280 Sir Will* Yonge,* a politician
and versifier *280 Bubo* Dodington* *287–304* the eight 'who' clauses anticipate
'babbling blockheads'

Who has the Vanity to call you Friend,   295
Yet wants the Honour injured to defend;
Who tells whate'er you think, whate'er you say,
And, if he lie not, must at least betray;
Who to the *Dean* and *silver Bell* can swear,
And sees at *Canons* what was never there: 300
Who reads, but with a Lust to misapply,
Makes Satire a Lampoon, and Fiction, Lie;
A Lash like mine no honest man shall dread,
But all such babbling blockheads in his stead.
    Let *Sporus* tremble— 'What? that thing of silk,   305
Sporus, that mere white Curd of Ass's milk?
Satire or Sense, alas! can *Sporus* feel,
Who breaks a Butterfly upon a Wheel?'
    Yet let me flap this Bug with gilded wings,
This painted Child of Dirt that stinks and stings;   310
Whose Buzz the Witty and the Fair annoys,
Yet Wit ne'er tastes, and Beauty ne'er enjoys:
So well-bred Spaniels civilly delight
In mumbling of the Game they dare not bite.
Eternal Smiles his Emptiness betray,   315
As shallow streams run dimpling all the way.
Whether in florid Impotence he speaks,
And, as the Prompter breathes, the Puppet squeaks;
Or at the Ear of *Eve*, familiar Toad!
Half Froth, half Venom, spits himself abroad,   320
In Puns, or Politics, or Tales, or Lies,
Or Spite, or Smut, or Rhymes, or Blasphemies.
His Wit all see-saw, between *that* and *this*,
Now high, now low, now Master up, now Miss,
And he himself one vile Antithesis.   325

299–300 see *To Burlington* 141–50 (p. 119) *305 Sporus* name of Nero's eunuch and minion; here applied to Hervey* *thing* i.e. neither man nor woman *306 ass's milk* prescribed for invalids *310 painted* made-up, and coloured like a dung-beetle *319 toad* from *Paradise Lost* iv 800 *325 antithesis* complex pun on the contradictions of his character and the 'see-saw' of his wit

134

Amphibious Thing! that acting either Part,
The trifling Head, or the corrupted Heart;
Fop at the Toilet, Flatt'rer at the Board,
Now trips a Lady, and now struts a Lord.
Eve's Tempter thus the Rabbins have expressed,　　　330
A Cherub's face, a Reptile all the rest.
Beauty that shocks you, Parts that none will trust,
Wit that can creep, and Pride that licks the dust.
　　Not Fortune's Worshipper, nor Fashion's fool,
Not Lucre's Madman, nor Ambition's Tool,　　　335
Not proud, nor servile; be one Poet's praise,
That, if he pleased, he pleased by manly ways:　　[Pope himself]
That Flattery, even to Kings, he held a shame,
And thought a Lie in Verse or Prose the same;
That not in Fancy's maze he wandered long,　　　340
But stooped to Truth, and moralized his song:
That not for Fame, but Virtue's better end,
He stood the furious Foe, the timid friend,
The damning Critic, half-approving Wit,
The Coxcomb hit, or fearing to be hit;　　　345
Laughed at the loss of Friends he never had,
The dull, the proud, the wicked, and the mad;
The distant Threats of Vengeance on his head,
The Blow unfelt, the Tear he never shed;
The Tale revived, the Lie so oft o'erthrown,　　　350
Th' imputed Trash, and Dulness not his own;
The Morals blacken'd when the Writings 'scape,
The libell'd Person, and the pictured Shape;
Abuse, on all he loved, or loved him, spread,
A Friend in Exile, or a Father, dead;　　　355

---

328 board council or dinner table *330 Rabbins* Jewish theologians *341 stooped to truth* like a falcon to its lure *351 imputed trash* e.g. work attributed to Pope by Curll* *353 person* i.e. Pope's own *pictured shape* caricature *355 friend in exile* Atterbury*

The Whisper, that to Greatness still too near, *[Hervey]*
Perhaps, yet vibrates on his SOVEREIGN's ear—
Welcome for thee, fair Virtue! all the past:
For thee, fair Virtue! welcome ev'n the *last*!

  'But why insult the Poor, affront the Great?'   360
A Knave's a Knave, to me, in every State;
Alike my scorn, if he succeed or fail, *[Japhet had his ears cut for fraud]*
Sporus at Court, or *Japhet* in a Jail,
A hireling Scribbler, or a hireling Peer,
Knight of the Post corrupt, or of the Shire,   365
If on a Pillory, or near a Throne, *[deceived person]*
He gain his Prince's Ear, or lose his own.
  Yet soft by Nature, more a Dupe than Wit,
Sappho can tell you how this Man was bit:
This dreaded Sat'rist *Dennis* will confess   370
Foe to his Pride, but Friend to his Distress: *[Pope had helped him]*
So humble, he has knocked at *Tibbald's* door,
Has drunk with *Cibber*, nay has rhymed for *Moore*. *[Smythe]*
Full ten years slandered, did he once reply?
Three thousand Suns went down on *Welsted's* Lie;   375
To please a *Mistress*, One aspersed his life; *[William Windham]*
He lashed him not, but let her be his *Wife*:
Let *Budgell* charge low *Grub Street* on his quill
And write whate'er he pleased, except his *Will*;
Let the *Two Curlls* of town and court abuse   380
His Father, Mother, Body, Soul, and Muse.
Yet why? that Father held it for a rule,
It was a Sin to call our Neighbour Fool:
That harmless Mother thought no Wife a Whore:
Hear this, and spare his Family, *James Moore*!   385

356 whisper i.e. Hervey *363 Japhet* Crook* *365 Knight of the post* professionally corrupt witness *368 dupe* i.e. 'this man', bitten by Lady Montagu's (Sappho's) wit *373 Moore* Smythe* *374 ten years* i.e. before *The Dunciad* *375 Welsted* first attacked Pope in 1717 *376 Mistress* Mary Howard* *378 Budgell* forged a will and attributed to Pope some comments on the matter in the *Grubstreet Journal* *380 two Curlls* Curll* and Hervey*, who both jeered at Pope's family

Unspotted Names! and memorable long,
If there be Force in Virtue, or in Song.
    Of gentle Blood (part shed in Honour's Cause,
While yet in *Britain* Honour had Applause)
Each parent sprung—'What fortune, pray?'— Their own,   390
And better got than *Bestia*'s from the Throne.
Born to no Pride, inheriting no Strife,
Nor marrying Discord in a Noble Wife,
Stranger to Civil and Religious Rage,
The good Man walked innoxious through his Age.   395
No Courts he saw, no Suits would ever try,
Nor dared an Oath, nor hazarded a Lie.
Unlearn'd, he knew no Schoolman's subtle Art,
No Language, but the Language of the Heart.
By Nature honest, by Experience wise,   400
Healthy by Temp'rance, and by Exercise:
His Life, though long, to sickness passed unknown,
His Death was instant, and without a groan.
O grant me thus to live, and thus to die!
Who sprung from Kings shall know less joy than I.   405
O Friend! may each Domestic Bliss be thine!
Be no unpleasing Melancholy mine:
Me, let the tender Office long engage,
To rock the Cradle of reposing Age,
With lenient Arts extend a Mother' breath,   410
Make Languor smile, and smooth the Bed of Death.
Explore the Thought, explain the asking Eye,
And keep awhile one Parent from the Sky!
On Cares like these if Length of days attend,
May Heaven, to bless those days, preserve my Friend,   415

---

391 Bestia a corrupt consul, for Marlborough (?) *393 marrying discord* Dryden
and Addison both married 'noble' wives and suffered 'discord'. *410 lenient* sooth-
ing *414 attend* wait upon

Preserve him social, cheerful, and serene,
And just as rich as when he served a QUEEN.
Whether that Blessing be denied, or given,
Thus far was right, the rest belongs to Heaven.

SATIRES AND EPISTLES OF
HORACE IMITATED

Pope prefaced the 1735 edition of his *Satires* (which included some modernizations of Donne) with this advertisement:

> The occasion of publishing these *Imitations* was the clamour raised on some of my *Epistles*. And answer from *Horace* was both more full, and of more dignity, than any I could have made in my own person; and the example of much greater freedom in so eminent a Divine as *Dr Donne*, seemed a proof with what indignation and contempt a Christian may treat vice or folly, in ever so low, or ever so high, a station. Both these authors were acceptable to the Princes and Ministers under whom they lived: *The Satires of Dr Donne* I versified at the desire of the Earl of Oxford while he was Lord Treasurer, and of the Duke of Shrewsbury who had been Secretary of State; neither of whom looked upon a satire on vicious courts as any reflection on those they served in. And indeed there is not in the world a greater error, than that which fools are so apt to fall into, and knaves with good reason to encourage, the mistaking a *Satirist* for a *Libeller*; whereas to a *true Satirist* nothing is so odious as a *Libeller*, for the same reason as to a man *truly Virtuous* nothing is so hateful as a *Hypocrite*.

In naming the Earl of Oxford and the Duke of Shrewsbury Pope is looking back, ironically and provocatively, to the Tory administration that had collapsed with the death of Queen Anne

---

417 rich richly endowed *served a queen* Arbuthnot was displaced at court on the death of Queen Anne in 1714. The Whigs, suffering only minor setbacks and never losing their hold in Parliament, were to stay in power until 1761.

By far the greatest of the dispossesed Tories still active in the 1730s was Henry St John, Viscount Bolingbroke, and in a sense he may be said to preside over this group of satires. Bolingbroke is said to have suggested the imitation of Book II Satire 1 when he called on Pope as a sick-visitor; the imitation of Book I Epistle 1 is addressed to him, and it was he who supplied (through his *Dissertation on Parties*) most of the political ideas of Pope's *Epilogue*.

The triumph of the *Imitations*, however, is in their assimilation of Pope's feelings and thoughts about the contemporary world (whether characteristically Tory or not) into the very fabric of Horace's verse. Pope's versions were published alongside the Latin original, and their wit is largely in the completeness with which Horace's Rome is transposed to Pope's London, the *pax Augustina* to the *pax Walpoliana*. The trick had been played before (notably, as Dr Johnson says, by Oldham and Rochester) but never before, or since, with such authority, skill and conviction.

To Mr Fortescue (Horace, *Satires* II 1)

With a perverse pride, perhaps, Pope called this piece (the first occasioned by Bolingbroke's visit to his sickroom in 1733) 'a slight thing, the work of two days'. In the poem that Pope is imitating, Horace 'supposes himself to consult with Trebatius, whether he should desist from writing satires or not'. The *Imitation* is therefore an apt prologue to the *Satires*, and it is only partially displaced in this role by the more elaborately wrought epistle to Arbuthnot. It was first associated in public with the distinguished lawyer and Master of the Rolls, William Fortescue, by Warburton in 1751; but Pope had written to Fortescue in 1733 saying that he had begun with the intention of making him Trebatius but before he came to the end he 'considered it might be too ludicrous'. The ascription is retained here as a convenient title. The Friend represents a kind of ironic worldliness that Pope refuses to reconcile with the true functions of a satirist. The tone echoes the Horatian original—good humoured in its manner of address to the friend, and truculent in its passing indictments of society at large.

The capitalization of the 1734 edition is here much reduced.

TO MR FORTESCUE

(Horace, *Satires* II 1)

P. THERE are (I scarce can think it, but am told,
There are, to whom my satire seems too bold:
Scarce to wise *Peter* complaisant enough,
And something said of *Chartres* much too rough.
The lines are weak, another's pleased to say,   5
Lord *Fanny* spins a thousand such a day.
Tim'rous by nature, of the rich in awe,
I come to Counsel learned in the law:
You'll give me, like a friend both sage and free,
Advice; and (as you use) without a fee.   10
    F. I'd write no more.
                        P. Not write? but then I *think*,
And for my soul I cannot sleep a wink:
I nod in company, I wake at night,
Fools rush into my head, and so I write.
    F. You could not do a worse thing for your life.   15
Why, if the nights seem tedious—take a wife;
Or rather truly, if your point be rest,
Lettuce and cowslip wine; *Probatum est.*

3 *Peter* Walter* 6 *Fanny* Hervey* 18 *lettuce and cowslip wine* said to quieten passion and induce sleep *probatum est* 'it is proved'; a legal formula

But talk with *Celsus*, *Celsus* will advise
Hartshorn, or something that shall close your eyes.   20
Or, if you needs must write, write Cæsar's praise,
You'll gain at least a *Knighthood* or the *Bays*.

   P. What! like Sir *Richard*, rumbling, rough, and fierce,
With Arms and George and Brunswick crowd the verse?
Rend with tremendous sound your ears asunder,   25
With gun, drum, trumpet, blunderbuss, and thunder?
Or, nobly wild, with *Budgell's* fire and force,
Paint angels trembling round his falling horse?

   F. Then all your Muse's softer art display,
Let *Carolina* smooth the tuneful lay,   30
Lull with *Amelia's* liquid name the Nine,
And sweetly flow through all the Royal Line.

   P. Alas! few verses touch their nicer ear;
They scarce can bear their *Laureate* twice a year;
And justly Cæsar scorns the poet's lays,—   35
It is to *History* he trusts for praise.

   F. Better be *Cibber*, I'll maintain it still,
Than ridicule all *Taste*, blaspheme *Quadrille*,
Abuse the City's best good men in metre,
And laugh at Peers that put their trust in Peter.   40
Even those you touch not, hate you.
                     P. What should ail t'em?

   F. A hundred smart in *Timon* and in *Balaam*:
The fewer still you name, you wound the more;
Bond is but one, but *Harpax* is a score.

   P. Each mortal has his pleasure: none deny   45
Scarsdale his bottle, *Darty* his ham-pie;

---

19 *Celsus* Roman physician 20 *hartshorn* ammonia; thought soporific 22 *bays* laureateship 23 *Sir Richard* Blackmore* 27 *Budgell** wrote of the death of George II's horse in battle, but without 'angels' 30 *Carolina*, *Amelia* the Queen and princess 34 *Laureate* i.e. Cibber* 34 *twice a year* new-year and the King's birthday 42–4 for Pope's use of these names see pp. 101, 109, 117) 46 *Scarsdale* Nicholas Leke, a Tory peer *Darty* Charles Dartineuf, a notable epicure.

Ridotta sips and dances, till she see
The doubling lustres dance as fast as she;
F—— loves the *Senate*, *Hockley-hole* his brother,
Like, in all else, as one egg to another.   50
I love to pour out all myself, as plain
As downright *Shippen*, or as old *Montaigne*.
In them, as certain to be loved as seen,
The Soul stood forth, nor kept a thought within;
In me what spots (for spots I have) appear,   55
Will prove at least the medium must be clear.
In this impartial glass, my Muse intends
Fair to expose myself, my foes, my friends;
Publish the present age; but, where my text
Is vice too high, reserve it for the next: 60
My foes shall wish my life a longer date,
And every friend the less lament my fate.

   My Head and Heart thus flowing through my quill,
Verse-man or Prose-man, term me which you will,
Papist or Protestant, or both between,   65
Like good *Erasmus* in an honest mean,
In Moderation placing all my Glory,
While Tories call me Whig, and Whigs a Tory.

   Satire's my weapon, but I'm too discreet
To run a-muck, and tilt at all I meet;   70
I only wear it in a land of hectors,
Thieves, Supercargoes, Sharpers, and Directors.
Save but our *Army*! and let *Jove* incrust
Swords, pikes, and guns, with everlasting rust!
Peace is my dear delight—not *Fleury's* more: 75

47 Ridotta 'society woman'; from 'ridotto', a party *48 lustres* chandeliers *49*
Stephen Fox* enjoyed Parliament, Henry enjoyed the Bear-garden *52 Shippen* a
notably honest Jacobite M.P. *61–2* i.e. the vicious will feel safe until after Pope's
death and friends need not fret about his persecution *64 verse-man* Bathurst* called
Prior his verse-man and Lewis his prose-man; Pope serves no patron but his 'head
and heart' *71 hectors* street bullies *72 supercargoes* cargo supervisors—notoriously
rich *directors* see p. 102 *73 our army* i.e. the forces of sature, with glance at Walpole's standing army

But touch me, and no Minister so sore.
Whoe'er offends, at some unlucky time
Slides into verse, and hitches in a rhyme,
Sacred to Ridicule! his whole life long,
And the sad burthen of some merry song.   80

    Slander or Poison, dread from *Delia's* rage,
Hard words or Hanging, if your Judge be *Page*.
From furious *Sappho* scarce a milder Fate,
Poxed by her Love, or libelled by her Hate.
Its proper power to hurt, each creature feels;   85
Bulls aim their horns, and Asses lift their heels;
'Tis a bear's talent not to kick, but hug;
And no man wonders he's not stung by Pug:
So drink with *Walters,* or with *Chartres* eat,
They'll never poison you, they'll only cheat.   90

    Then, learned Sir! (to cut the matter short)
Whate'er my fate, or well or ill at Court;
Whether old age, with faint but cheerful ray,
Attends to gild the evening of my day,
Or death's black wing already be display'd,   95
To wrap me in the universal shade;
Whether the darken'd room to Muse invite,
Or whiten'd wall provoke the skewer to write:
In durance, exile, Bedlam, or the Mint,
Like *Lee* or *Budgell*, I will rhyme and print.   100

    F. Alas young man! your days can ne'er be long,
In flower of age you perish for a song!
Plums and directors, Shylock and his wife,
Will club their testers, now, to take your life!

    P. What! armed for *Virtue*, when I point the pen,   105
Brand the bold front of shameless, guilty men;

---

78 i.e. gets caught up in the satirist's verse *81 Delia* Mary Howard* *83 Sappho*
Lady Montagu* *99 mint* sanctuary for debtors *103 plums* men worth £100,000
Shylock see p. 101, 102 *104 testers* 'sixpences' *105 point* sharpen; direct like a
sword *106 front* forehead; front-line

Dash the proud gamester in his gilded car;
Bare the mean heart that lurks beneath a Star;
Can there be wanting, to defend her Cause,
Lights of the Church, or Guardians of the Laws?   110
Could pensioned *Boileau* lash in honest strain
Flatterers and bigots even in *Louis*' reign?
Could Laureate *Dryden* pimp and friar engage,
Yet neither *Charles* nor *James* be in a rage?
And I not strip the gilding off a knave,   115
Unplaced, unpensioned, no man's heir, or slave?
I will, or perish in the gen'rous Cause.
Hear this and tremble! you, who 'scape the Laws:
Yes, while I live, no rich or noble knave
Shall walk the world, in credit, to his grave.   120
To VIRTUE ONLY, AND HER FRIENDS, A FRIEND:
The World beside may murmur, or commend.
Know, all the distant din that world can keep,
Rolls o'er my *Grotto*, and but soothes my sleep.
There, my retreat the best companions grace,   125
Chiefs, out of War, and Statesmen, out of Place.
There St John mingles with my friendly bowl
The Feast of Reason and the Flow of Soul:
And he, whose lightning pierced the *Iberian* lines,
Now forms my quincunx, and now ranks my vines,   130
Or tames the genius of the stubborn plain,
Almost as quickly as he conquered *Spain*.
  Envy must own, I live among the Great,
No pimp of pleasure, and no spy of state,
With eyes that pry not, tongue that ne'er repeats,   135
Fond to spread friendships, but to cover heats;

107 car coach; chariot *108 star* badge of Knighthood *111 Boileau* wrote *Le Lutrin* under Louis XIV *113 Dryden* wrote *The Spanish Friar* which was in fact banned by James II. *116 un-pensioned* Pope twice refused a pension. *117 generous* noble *124 grotto* built under the main road dividing Pope's Twickenham grounds *127 St John* Bolingbroke* *129* Mordaunt, Earl of Peterborough, a general in the Spanish campaign 1705 *136 cover heats* conceal quarrels

To help who want, to forward who excel;—
This, all who know me, know; who love me, tell:
And who unknown defame me, let them be
Scribblers or peers, alike are *Mob* to me.   140
This is my plea, on this I rest my Cause—
What saith my Counsel, learned in the Laws?

   F. Your plea is good. But still I say, beware!
Laws are explained by men—so have a care.
It stands on record, that in *Richard's* times   145
A man was hanged for very honest rhymes;
Consult the statute: *quart.* I think it is,
Edwardi Sext. or *prim. et quint. Eliz.*
See *Libels, Satires*—here you have it—read.

   P. Libels and *Satires*! lawless things indeed!   150
But grave *Epistles*, bringing vice to light,
Such as a *King* might read, a *Bishop* write;
Such as *Sir Robert* would approve—

                              F. Indeed!

The case is altered—you may then proceed;
In such a Cause the Plaintiff will be hissed,   155
My Lords the Judges laugh, and you're dismissed.

To Mr. Bethel (Horace, *Satires* II 2)
Hugh Bethel was a landed gentleman from the East Riding of
Yorkshire. Pope valued his friendship and appreciated the plain
sufficiency of his hospitality; he associated Bethel's name with the
poem from the beginning (substituting it for that of Horace's
Ofellus) but the dedication belongs to 1751.

   As in the Epistles to Bathurst and Burlington, Pope is here
concerned that wealth should honour its obligations, and that the

146 a man was hanged by Richard III, for a seditious couplet *147–8* references to
the libel laws *153 Sir Robert* Walpole*

way of life it supports should conform to the central virtues of humane, temperate living.

The capitalization is that of the 1734 edition.

TO MR BETHEL

(Horace, *Satires* II 2)

WHAT, and how great, the Virtue and the Art
To live on little with a cheerful heart,
(A Doctrine sage, but truly none of mine);
Let's talk, my friends, but talk before we dine.
Not when a gilt Buffet's reflected pride   5
Turns you from sound Philosophy aside;
Not when from Plate to Plate your eyeballs roll,
And the brain dances to the mantling bowl.
  Hear Bethel's Sermon, one not versed in schools,
But strong in sense, and wise without the rules.   10
  Go work, hunt, exercise! (he thus began)
Then scorn a homely dinner, if you can.
Your wine locked up, your Butler strolled abroad,
Or fish denied (the river yet unthawed)
If then plain Bread and Milk will do the feat,   15
The pleasure lies in *you*, and not the meat.
Preach as I please, I doubt our curious men
Will choose a *Pheasant* still before a *Hen;*
Yet hens of *Guinea* full as good I hold,
Except you eat the feathers, green and gold.   20
Of *Carps* and *Mullets* why prefer the *great*
(Though cut in pieces ere my Lord can eat),
Yet for *small Turbots* such esteem profess?
Because God made these large, the other less.

8 mantling bowl frothing punch-bowl *17 curious* of refined taste

Oldfield with more than Harpy throat endued, 25
Cries, 'Send me, gods! a whole hog *barbecued*!'
Oh, blast it, South winds! till a stench exhale
Rank as the ripeness of a Rabbit's tail.
By what *Criterion* do you eat, d'ye think,
If this is prized for *sweetness*, that for *stink*? 30
When the tired Glutton labours through a Treat,
He finds no relish in the sweetest Meat;
He calls for something bitter, something sour,
And the rich feast concludes extremely poor:
Cheap eggs, and herbs, and olives still we see, 35
Thus much is left of old Simplicity!
    The *Robin redbreast* till of late had rest,
And children sacred held a *Martin's* nest,
Till *Beccaficos* sold so devilish dear
To one that was, or would have been a Peer. 40
Let me extol a *Cat* on Oysters fed,
I'll have a Party at the *Bedford Head*,
Or e'en to crack live *Crawfish* recommend;
I'd never doubt at Court to make a Friend.
    'Tis yet in vain, I own, to keep a pother 45
About one Vice, and fall into the other:
Between Excess and Famine lies a mean;
Plain, but not sordid, though not splendid, clean.
    Avidien, or his Wife (no matter which,
For him you'll call a dog, and her a bitch) 50
Sell their presented Partridges, and Fruits,
And humbly live on rabbits and on roots:
One half-pint bottle serves them both to dine,
And is at once their vinegar and wine.

---

26 barbecued 'A West Indian term of gluttony; a hog roasted whole, stuffed with spice, and basted with Madeira wine' (Pope). *39 beccafico* Italian 'fig-pecker', a delicacy in autumn when fed on figs and grapes *42 Bedford Head* an eating house *49 Avidien* from Horace, applied to Montagu*

But on some lucky day (as when they found   55
A lost Bank-bill, or heard their Son was drowned),
At such a feast old vinegar to spare,
Is what two souls so generous cannot bear:
Oil, though it stink, they drop by drop impart,
But souse the Cabbage with a bounteous heart.   60

  He knows to live, who keeps the middle state,
And neither leans on this side nor on that:
Nor stops, for one bad Cork, his Butler's pay,
Swears, like Albutius, a good Cook away;
Nor lets, like Nævius, every error pass,   65
The musty wine, foul cloth, or greasy glass.

  Now hear what blessings Temperance can bring:
(Thus said our Friend, and what he said I sing).
First health: the stomach (crammed from every dish,
A tomb of boiled and roast, and flesh and fish,   70
Where Bile, and wind, and phlegm, and acid jar,
And all the Man is one intestine war),
Remembers oft the School-boy's simple fare,
The temperate sleeps, and spirits light as air.

  How pale each Worshipful and reverend Guest   75
Rise from a Clergy, or a City, feast!
What life in all that ample Body, say?
What heavenly Particle inspires the clay?
The Soul subsides, and wickedly inclines
To seem but mortal, even in sound Divines.   80
On morning wings how active springs the Mind
That leaves the load of yesterday behind!
How easy every labour it pursues!
How coming to the Poet every Muse!

57 spare be sparing with (?) *60 souse* i.e. in vinegar *63 bad cork* spoils the wine
64–5 Albutius, Nævius types from Horace *68 Friend* Horace *72 intestine* puns on
sense 'civil' *77 ample body* large gathering; gross bellied man *78 inspires* breathes
life into *79 subsides* when by nature it should rise *inclines* bends downwards *80
sound divines* orthodox clergymen, believing the soul cannot die *81–4* ironical
treatment of the morning after

Not but we may exceed, some Holy time,   85
Or tired in search of Truth, or search of Rhyme;
Ill-health some just indulgence may engage;
And more, the Sickness of long Life, Old-age:
For fainting Age what cordial drop remains,
If our intemperate Youth the Vessel drains?   90
   Our Fathers praised rank ven'son. You suppose,
Perhaps, young men! our Fathers had no nose?
Not so: a Buck was then a week's repast,
And 'twas their point, I ween, to make it last:
More pleased to keep it till their friends could come,   95
Than eat the sweetest by themselves at home.
Why had not I in those good times my birth,
Ere Coxcomb-pies or Coxcombs were on earth?
   Unworthy He, the voice of Fame to hear,
(That sweetest Music to an honest ear   100
For 'faith, Lord Fanny! you are in the wrong,
The World's good word is better than a Song);
Who has not learned fresh Sturgeon and Ham-pie
Are no rewards for Want and Infamy!
When Luxury has licked up all thy pelf,   105
Cursed by thy neighbours, thy Trustees, thyself,
To friends, to fortune, to mankind a shame,
Think how Posterity will treat thy name;
And buy a Rope, that future times may tell
Thou has at least bestowed one penny well.   110
   'Right,' cries his Lordship, 'for a Rogue in need
To have a Taste, is Insolence indeed:
In me 'tis noble, suits my birth and state,
My wealth unwieldy, and my heap too great.'
Then, like the Sun, let Bounty spread her ray,   115
And shine that Superfluity away.

89 cordial stimulating *98 coxcomb* cock's comb, used as garnish; fool, from the shape of a jester's cap *101–2* Hervey's saying is lost. *104 rewards* recompenses *105 pelf* filthy lucre *106 trustees* creditors (?)

Oh Impudence of wealth! with all thy store,
How darest thou let one worthy man be poor?
Shall half the new-built Churches round thee fall?
Make Quays, build Bridges, or repair Whitehall: 120
Or to thy Country let that heap be lent,
As M**o's was, but not at five *per cent.*

    Who thinks that Fortune cannot change her mind,
Prepares a dreadful Jest for all mankind!
And who stands safest, tell me? is it he   125
That spreads and swells in puffed Prosperity;
Or blest with little, whose preventing care
In Peace provides fit arms against a War?

    Thus Bethel spoke, who always speaks his thought,
And always thinks the very thing he ought: 130
His equal mind I copy what I can,
And, as I love, would imitate the Man.
In *South-sea* days not happier, when surmised
The Lord of thousands, than if now *Excised*;
In Forest planted by a Father's hand,   135
Than in five acres now of rented land.
Content with little, I can piddle here
On broccoli and mutton, round the year;
But ancient friends (though poor, or out of play)
That touch my Bell, I canot turn away.   140
'Tis true, no Turbots dignify my boards,
But gudgeons, flounders, what my Thames affords.
To Hounslow Heath I point, and Bansted Down,
Thence comes your mutton, and these chicks my own:
From yon old walnut-tree a shower shall fall;   145
And grapes, long lingering on my only wall,

---

119 see p. 120 *122* *M**o* Duchess of Marlborough, who in fact reduced her loans
to the government from six to four per cent *131* *equal* equitable; equable *133*
South-Sea Pope lost money in the South Sea Bubble *134* *excised* Walpole had
proposed a general excise. *135* *forest* Binfield, in Windsor Forest *136* *five acres*
at Twickenham *137* *piddle* toy with food

And figs from standard and Espalier join;
The devil is in you if you cannot dine:
Then cheerful healths (your Mistress shall have place),
And, what's more rare, a Poet shall say *Grace*.   150
Fortune not much of humbling me can boast:
Though double-taxed, how little have I lost?
My Life's amusements have been just the same,
Before, and after Standing Armies came.
My lands are sold, my Father's house is gone;   155
I'll hire another's, is not that my own,
And yours, my friends? through whose free opening gate
None comes too early, none departs too late;
(For I, who hold sage Homer's rule the best,
Welcome the coming, speed the going guest).   160
'Pray Heaven it last! (cries Swift!) as you go on;
I wish to God this house had been you own:
Pity! to build without a son or wife:
Why, you'll enjoy it only all your life.'
Well, if the Use be mine, can it concern one,   165
Whether the Name belong to Pope or Vernon?
What's *Property*? dear Swift! you see it alter
From you to me, from me to Peter Walter:
Or, in a mortgage, prove a Lawyer's share;
Or, in a jointure, vanish from the Heir;   170
Or, in pure Equity (the Case not clear)
The Chancery takes your rents for twenty year:
At best, it falls to some ungracious Son,
Who cries, 'My father's damned, and all's my own.'
Shades, that to Bacon could retreat afford,   175
Become the portion of a booby Lord;

147 espalier lattice-trained tree *149 healths* toasts *152 double-taxed* extra taxes were
imposed on Catholics in 1715 *154 standing armies* maintained since 1688 *160* a line
in Pope's *Odyssey* (xv 84) *161 as you go on* when you depart this life *166 Vernon*
Mrs Vernon owned the Twickenham house. *170 jointure* estate willed to wife
and apt to pass to her side of the family *171 Equity* principles of law, administered
by Court of Chancery *176 booby Lord* Grimston*

And Helmsley once proud Buckingham's delight,
Slides to a Scrivener or a City Knight:
Let Lands and Houses have what Lords they will,
Let Us be fixed, and our own Masters still.   180

To Lord Bolingbroke (Horace, *Epistles* I 1)

Bolingbroke, as the wisest and noblest of Pope's mentors, is
chosen to stand for Horace's patron Maecenas. As Bolingbroke
had retired to France in 1735 this Epistle (1738) might more
readily be taken as a gird at the Walpole regime. But, more
fundamentally, it is about the possibility of attaining maturity
and wisdom in age, under the stresses of a hostile state of
civilization. The processes of growth do not readily promise a
ripe harvest, but take ugly, inhuman and parasitic forms:

> Some with fat Bucks on childless Dotards fawn;
> Some win rich Widows by their Chine and Brawn;
> While with the silent growth of ten per cent.,
> In Dirt and darkness, hundreds stink content.

There is a strong Stoic strain in the resolution of the poem but its
assertions of human dignity are undermined by the last line: the
poet cannot become the 'Man divine' that Bolingbroke seeks to
make him—his constitution is too vulnerable:

> Nay half in Heaven—except (what's mighty odd)
> A Fit of Vapours clouds this Demi-god.

The capitilization follows the 1738 edition.

---

177 *Helmsley* the Duke of Buckingham's home, sold to Sir Charles Duncombe
a London banker

TO LORD BOLINGBROKE

(Horace, *Epistles* I 1)

ST. JOHN, whose love indulged my labours past,
Matures my present, and shall bound my last!
Why will you break the Sabbath of my days?
Now sick alike of Envy and of Praise.
Public too long, ah, let me hide my Age!   5
See modest Cibber now has left the Stage:
Our Gen'rals now, retired to their Estates,
Hang their old Trophies o'er the Garden gates;
In Life's cool evening satiate of applause,
Nor fond of bleeding, even in BRUNSWICK's cause.   10
    A Voice there is, that whispers in my ear
('Tis Reason's voice, which sometimes one can hear),
'Friend Pope! be prudent, let your Muse take breath,
And never gallop Pegasus to death;
Lest stiff, and stately, void of fire or force,   15
You limp, like Blackmore on a Lord Mayor's horse.'
    Farewell then Verse, and Love, and every Toy.
The rhymes and rattles of the Man or Boy;
What right, what true, what fit, we justly call,
Let this be all my care—for this is All: 20
To lay this harvest up, and hoard with haste
What ev'ry day will want, and most, the last.
    But ask not, to what Doctors I apply?
Sworn to no Master, of no Sect am I:
As drives the storm, at any door I knock,   25
And house with Montaigne now, or now with Locke;

1 St John Bolingbroke* *2 bound* mark the end and purpose of *3 break the Sabbath*
i.e. 'occasion verse from me when I ought to be resting' Pope had turned forty-
nine, sometimes regarded as a Sabbath year; *16 Blackmore** alluding to the gait
of his verse

Sometimes a Patriot, active in debate,
Mix with the World, and battle for the State,
Free as young Lyttleton, her cause pursue,
Still true to Virtue, and as warm as true;   30
Sometimes with Aristippus, or St Paul,
Indulge my Candour, and grow all to all;
Back to my native Moderation slide,
And win my way by yielding to the tide.

    Long, as to him who works for debt, the Day,   35
Long as the Night to her whose love's away,
Long as the Year's dull circle seems to run,
When the brisk Minor pants for twenty-one;
So slow the unprofitable Moments roll,
That lock up all the Functions of my soul;   40
That keep me from Myself; and still delay
Life's instant business to a future day:
That task, which as we follow, or despise,
The eldest is a fool, the youngest wise:
Which done, the poorest can no wants endure,   45
And which not done, the richest must be poor.

    Late as it is, I put myself to school,
And feel some comfort, not to be a fool.
Weak though I am of limb, and short of sight,
Far from a Lynx, and not a Giant quite;   50
I'll do what MEAD and CHESELDEN advise,
To keep these limbs, and to preserve these eyes.
Not to go back, is somewhat to advance,
And men must walk at least before they dance.

    Say, does thy blood rebel, thy bosom move   55
With wretched Av'rice, or as wretched Love?

---

27 patriot opposition member *31 Aristippus* forerunner of Epicurus; Boling-broke's favourite philosopher *St Paul* see I Cor. ix 22 *32 candour* impartiality *41 still* continually *42 instant* urgent, vital *43 that task* i.e. the harvesting of virtue *45 endure* suffer

Know, there are Words, and Spells, which can control
(Between the Fits) this Fever of the soul:
Know, there are Rhymes, which (fresh and fresh applied)
Will cure the arrant'st Puppy of his Pride.   60
Be furious, envious, slothful, mad or drunk,
Slave to a Wife, or Vassal to a Punk,
A Switz, a High-Dutch, or a Low-Dutch Bear;
All that we ask is but a patient Ear.
    'Tis the first Virtue, Vices to abhor: 65
And the first Wisdom, to be Fool no more.
But to the world no bugbear is so great,
As want of figure, and a small Estate.
To either India see the Merchant fly,
Scared at the spectre of pale Poverty!   70
See him, with pains of body, pangs of soul,
Burn through the Tropic, freeze beneath the Pole!
Wilt thou do nothing for a nobler end,
Nothing, to make Philosophy thy friend?
To stop thy foolish views, thy long desires,   75
And ease thy heart of all that it admires?
Here, Wisdom calls: 'Seek Virtue first! be bold!
As Gold to Silver, Virtue is to Gold.'
There, London's voice: 'Get Money, Money still!
And then let Virtue follow, if she will.'   80
This, this the saving doctrine, preach'd to all,
From low St James's up to high St Paul;
From him whose quill stands quiver'd at his ear,
To him who notches Sticks at Westminster.
    BARNARD in spirit, sense, and truth abounds;   85
'Pray, then, what wants he?' Fourscore thousand pounds;

---

63 *High-Dutch* South German *Low-Dutch* North German and Netherlandish
bear = boor, peasant (?) *68 figure* style of living *75 foolish views* idle visions *76
admires marvels at *82* referring to the High and Low parties in the English Church
83–4 contrast the low penman with the Exchequer clerk using tallies

A Pension, or such Harness for a slave
As Bug now has, and Dorimant would have.
BARNARD, thou art a Cit, with all thy worth;
But Bug and D*l, *their Honours*, and so forth.   90

Yet every child another song will sing,
'Virtue, brave boys! 'tis Virtue makes a King.'
True, conscious Honour is to feel no sin,
He's armed without that's innocent within;
Be this thy Screen, and this thy Wall of Brass;   95
Compared to this, a Minister's an Ass.

And say, to which shall our applause belong,
This new Court-jargon, or the good old song?
The modern language of corrupted Peers,
Or what was spoke at CRESSY and POITIERS?   100
Who counsels best? who whispers, 'Be but Great,
With Praise or Infamy, leave that to fate;
Get Place and Wealth, if possible with Grace;
If not, by any means get Wealth and Place.'
For what? to have a Box where Eunuchs sing,   105
And foremost in the Circle eye a King.
Or he, who bids thee face with steady view
Proud Fortune, and look shallow Greatness through:
And, while he bids thee, sets the Example too?
If such a Doctrine, in St James's air,   110
Should chance to make the well-dressed Rabble stare;
If honest S*z take scandal at a spark,
That less admires the Palace than the Park:
Faith, I shall give the answer Reynard gave:
'I cannot like, Dread Sir, your Royal Cave: 115
Because I see, by all the Tracks about,
Full many a Beast goes in, but none comes out.'

87 harness the Order of the Garter *88 Bug* Henry de Grey* *Dorimant* Etheridge's
Man of Mode *89 cit* city tradesman; commoner *90 D*l* Lord Delaval *95-6* a
glance at Walpole; see p. 177 *105 eunuchs* castrati, Italian opera-singers *107-9*
There are several triplets in this poem. *112 S*ʒ* Schutz, a courtier *spark* young
courtier *114 Reynard* i.e. the fox addressing the sick lion

Adieu to Virtue, if you're once a Slave:
Send her to Court, you send her to her Grave.
    Well, if a King's a Lion, at the least   120
The People are a many-headed Beast:
Can they direct what measures to pursue,
Who know themselves so little what to do?
Alike in nothing but one Lust of Gold,
Just half the land would buy, and half be sold: 125
Their Country's wealth our mightier Misers drain,
Or cross, to plunder Provinces, the Main;
The rest, some farm the Poor-box, some the Pews;
Some keep Assemblies, and would keep the Stews;
Some with fat Bucks on childless Dotards fawn;   130
Some win rich Widows by their Chine and Brawn;
While with the silent growth of ten per cent.,
In Dirt and darkness, hundreds stink content.
    Of all these ways, if each pursues his own,
Satire be kind, and let the wretch alone.   135
But show me one who has it in his power
To act consistent with himself an hour.
Sir Job sailed forth, the evening bright and still,
'No place on earth (he cried) like Greenwich hill!'
Up starts a Palace, lo, the obedient base   140
Slopes at its foot, the woods its sides embrace,
The silver Thames reflects its marble face.
Now let some whimsy, or that Devil within
Which guides all those who know not what they mean,
But give the Knight (or give his lady) spleen;   145
Away, away! take all your scaffolds down,
'For Snug's the word: My dear! we'll live in town.'

---

128 slave i.e. to the Court's influence *128 farm* lease to themselves; embezzle *128 pews* i.e. rent paid for pews *keep assemblies* attend or hold social gatherings *129 keep the stews* attend or own the brothels *131 chine and brawn* back-bone and muscle; contrasted with 'fat bucks' *133* alluding to bank-vaults *138 Sir Job* for Horace's 'Dives', and see Job i 10

At am'rous Flavio is the Stocking thrown?
That very night he longs to lie alone.
The Fool whose Wife elopes some thrice a quarter,   150
For matrimonial Solace dies a martyr.
Did ever Proteus, Merlin, any Witch,
Transform themselves so strangely as the Rich?
Well, but the Poor—the Poor have the same itch;
They change their weekly Barber, weekly News,   155
Prefer a new Japanner to their shoes,
Discharge their Garrets, move their Beds, and run
(They know not whither) in a Chaise and one;
They hire their Sculler, and, when once aboard,
Grow sick, and damn the Climate—like a Lord.   160
  You laugh, half Beau, half Sloven if I stand,
My Wig all powder, and all snuff my Band;
You laugh, if Coat and Breeches strangely vary,
White Gloves, and Linen worthy Lady Mary!
But, when no Prelate's Lawn with Hair-shirt lined   165
Is half so incoherent as my Mind;
When (each Opinion with the next at strife,
One ebb and flow of follies all my Life)
I plant, root up, I build, and then confound;
Turn round to square, and square again to round;   170
You never change one muscle of your face,
You think this Madness but a common case,
Nor once to Chanc'ry, not to Hale apply;
Yet hang your lip, to see a Seam awry!
Careless how ill I with myself agree,   17
Kind to my dress, my figure, not to Me.
Is this my Guide, Philosopher, and Friend?
This, He who loves me, and who ought to mend?

148 *stocking* the bride's—it was thrown to the wedding-guests and whoever was
hit was believed next to marry 151 'dies a witness to his faith in the comfort
of marriage' 156 *japanner* shoe-black 162 *band* neck-band 164 *Lady Mary* Lady
Montagu*; her linen was reputed dirty 165 *lawn* fine linen used for bishops'
sleeves

Who ought to make me (what he can, or none),
That Man divine whom Wisdom calls her own;   180
Great without Title, without Fortune blessed;
Rich, even when plundered, honoured while oppressed;
Loved without youth, and followed without power;
At home, though exiled—free, though in the Tower;
In short, that reas'ning, high, immortal Thing,   185
Just less than Jove, and much above a King,
Nay half in Heaven—except (what's mighty odd)
A Fit of Vapours clouds this Demi-god.

To Augustus (Horace, *Epistles* II i)
The pretences of Pope's age to call itself Augustan and assume
by imitation the literary and social glories of the age of Horace,
Virgil and Augustus Caesar are—in high Augustan style—most
severely called into question by this, the most elaborate and
most ambitious of the Epistles. George II's indifference to
the arts was (and remains) an excellent theme for indignation
and irony.

The traditions of English poetry, from Shakespeare to Swift,
have flourished in spite of the taste (for ribaldry, adulation and
farce) that the Court continued to promote. Pope's claims for the
poet range from the slyly modest ('What will a Child learn sooner
than a song?') to the momentous:

> And leave on *Swift* this grateful verse engraved,
> 'The Rights a Court attacked, a Poet saved.'
> Behold the hand that wrought a Nation's cure,
> Stretched to relieve the Idiot and the Poor.

But there is a consistent plea for continuity between what is to

188 vapours exhalations from the stomach, supposed to cause clouding of the
spirits; with suggestion of a monumental figure reaching into the clouds

be valued in the past, and what Pope acclaims in and near his own time:

> Britain to soft refinements less a foe,
> Wit grew polite, and Numbers learned to flow.
> Waller was smooth; but Dryden taught to join
> The varying verse, the full resounding line,
> The long majestic march, and energy divine.

Both by his argument and by his example Pope is setting up the standards by which the work of Ancients and Moderns must be judged.

The capitalization of the first edition is here considerably lightened.

TO AUGUSTUS

(Horace, *Epistles* II 1)

WHILE You, great Patron of Mankind, sustain
The balanced world, and open all the main;
Your Country, chief, in Arms abroad defend,
At home, with Morals, Arts, and Laws amend;
How shall the Muse from such a Monarch steal   5
An hour, and not defraud the Public Weal?
  Edward and Henry, now the boast of fame,
And virtuous Alfred, a more sacred name,
After a life of gen'rous toils endured,
The Gaul subdued, or Property secured,   10
Ambition humbled, mighty cities stormed,
Or Laws established, and the World reformed;

AUGUSTUS George II *2 open* i.e. to trade *7* Edward III and Henry V

Closed their long Glories with a sigh, to find
Th' unwilling Gratitude of base mankind!
All human Virtue, to its latest breath,   15
Finds Envy never conquered, but by Death.
The great Alcides, every labour passed,
Had still this Monster to subdue at last.
Sure fate of all, beneath whose rising ray
Each Star of meaner merit fades away!   20
Oppressed we feel the Beam directly beat,
Those Suns of Glory please not till they set.

    To Thee, the World its present homage pays,
The harvest early, but mature the praise:
Great Friend of LIBERTY! in *Kings* a Name   25
Above all Greek, above all Roman Fame:
Whose Word is Truth, as sacred and revered,
As Heaven's own Oracles from Altars heard.
Wonder of Kings! like whom, to mortal eyes
None e'er has risen, and none e'er shall rise.   30

    Just in one instance, be it yet confessed
Your People, Sir, are partial in the rest:
Foes to all living worth except your own,
And Advocates for Folly dead and gone.
Authors, like Coins, grow dear as they grow old;   35
It is the rust we value, not the gold.
Chaucer's worst ribaldry is learn'd by rote,
And beastly Skelton Heads of Houses quote;
One likes no language but the Faery Queen;
A Scot will fight for Christ's Kirk o' the Green: 40
And each true Briton is to Ben so civil,
He swears the Muses met him at the Devil.

---

38 Skelton Pope thought this lively Tudor poet 'scurrilous' when his work was reprinted in 1736. *Houses* colleges *40 Christ's Kirk* . . . ballad by James I or James V of Scotland; its advocate was Allan Ramsay *42 the Devil* Ben Jonson's tavern

Though justly Greece her eldest sons admires,
Why should not we be wiser than our Sires?
In every public Virtue we excel;   45
We build, we paint, we sing, we dance as well;
And learned Athens to our Art must stoop,
Could she behold us tumbling through a hoop.

If Time improve our Wit as well as Wine,
Say at what age a Poet grows divine?   50
Shall we, or shall we not, account him so,
Who died, perhaps, an hundred years ago?
End all dispute; and fix the year precise
When British bards begin t' Immortalise?

'Who lasts a Century can have no flaw,   55
I hold that Wit a Classic, good in law.'

Suppose he wants a year, will you compound?
And shall we deem him Ancient, right and sound,
Or damn to all Eternity at once,
At ninety-nine, a Modern, and a Dunce?   60

'We shall not quarrel for a year or two;
By Courtesy of England, he may do.'

Then, by the rule that made the Horse-tail bare,
I pluck out year by year, as hair by hair,
And melt down Ancients like a heap of snow: 65
While you, to measure merits, look in Stowe,
And estimating authors by the year,
Bestow a garland only on a bier.

Shakespeare (whom you and every play-house bill
Style the divine, the matchless, what you will),   70
For gain, not glory, winged his roving flight,
And grew Immortal in his own despite.
Ben, old and poor, as little seem'd to heed

---

48 alludes to the vogue for pantomime *62 Courtesy of England* a law by which a
widower was allowed his wife's property without prescriptive title *64 I pluck
out* i.e. read and judge for myself *66 Stowe* great Tudor chronicler

The Life to come, in every Poet's Creed.
Who now reads Cowley? if he pleases yet,   75
His moral pleases, not his pointed wit;
Forgot his Epic, nay Pindaric Art,
But still I love the language of his Heart.
   'Yet surely, surely, these were famous men!
What Boy but hears the sayings of old Ben?   80
In all debates where critics bear a part,
Not one but nods, and talks of Jonson's Art,
Of Shakespeare's Nature, and of Cowley's Wit;
How Beaumont's Judgment checked what Fletcher writ;
How Shadwell hasty, Wycherley was slow;   85
But, for the Passions, Southern sure and Rowe.
These, only these, support the crowded stage,
From eldest Heywood down to Cibber's age.'
   All this may be; the People's Voice is odd,
It is, and it is not, the voice of God.   90
To *Gammer Gurton* if it give the bays,
And yet deny the *Careless Husband* praise,
Or say our fathers never broke a rule;
Why then, I say, the Public is a fool.
But let them own, that greater faults than we   95
They had, and greater Virtues, I'll agree.
Spenser himself affects the obsolete,
And Sidney's verse halts ill on Roman feet:
Milton's strong pinion now not Heaven can bound,
Now serpent-like, in prose he sweeps the ground,   100
In Quibbles, Angel and Archangel join,
And God the Father turns a School-Divine.

---

74 life to come esteem of posterity, with glance at the catechism *85* Pope quotes
Rochester on Shadwell and Wycherley. *90 is . . . is not* perhaps, 'is potent but
not just' *91 Gammer Gurton* a Tudor comedy *92 Careless Husband* comedy by
Cibber* *97* a glance at the Chaucerian style of the Shepherd's Calendar *98 Roman
feet* Sidney tried Latin metres.

Not that I'd lop the Beauties from his book,
Like slashing Bentley with his desperate Hook,
Or damn all Shakespeare, like the affected fool   105
At Court, who hates whate'er he read at School.
   But for the Wits of either Charles's days,
The Mob of Gentlemen who wrote with Ease;
Sprat, Carew, Sedley, and a hundred more,
(Like twinkling stars the Miscellanies o'er)   110
One Simile, that solitary shines
In the dry Desert of a thousand lines,
Or lengthened Thought that gleams through many a page,
Has sanctified whole Poems for an age.
I lose my patience, and I own it too,   115
When works are censured, not as bad, but new;
While if our Elders break all Reason's laws,
These fools demand not Pardon, but Applause.
   On Avon's bank, where flowers eternal blow,
If I but ask, if any weed can grow?   120
One tragic sentence if I dare deride,
Which Betterton's grave action dignified,
Or well-mouthed Booth with emphasis proclaims
(Though but, perhaps, a muster-roll of names),
How will our Fathers rise up in a rage,   125
And swear, all shame is lost in George's Age!
You'd think no Fools disgraced the former reign,
Did not some grave Examples yet remain,
Who scorn a Lad should teach his Father skill,
And, having once been wrong, will be so still.   130
He, who to seem more deep than you or I,
Extols old Bards, or Merlin's prophecy,

---

104 Bentley* edited *Paradise Lost hook* square bracket used by Bentley to enclose
lines he thought spurious; pruning hook *110 Miscellanies* anthologies *120 weed*
Pope claimed to have rooted out wild and mean expressions in his edition of
Shakespeare. *122–3 Betterton, Booth* celebrated actors *132 Merlin* his role of
prophet was assumed by John Partridge in his Almanacs.

Mistake him not; he envies, not admires,
And to debase the Sons, exalts the Sires.
Had ancient Times conspired to disallow   135
What then was new, what had been ancient now?
Or what remained, so worthy to be read
By learned Critics, of the mighty Dead?
  In days of ease, when now the weary Sword
Was sheathed, and *Luxury* with *Charles* restored;   140
In every taste of foreign courts improved,
'All, by the King's Example, lived and loved.'
Then peers grew proud in Horsemanship t' excel,
Newmarket's Glory rose, as Britain's fell;
The Soldier breathed the Gallantries of France,   145
And every flowery Courtier writ Romance.
Then Marble, softened into life, grew warm,
And yielding Metal flowed to human form:
Lely on animated Canvas stole
The sleepy Eye, that spoke the melting soul.   150
No wonder then, when all was Love and Sport,
The willing Muses were debauched at Court:
On each enervate string they taught the Note
To pant, or tremble through an Eunuch's throat. But
  Britain, changeful as a Child at play,   155
Now calls in Princes, and now turns away.
Now Whig, now Tory, what we loved we hate;
Now all for Pleasure, now for Church and State;
Now for Prerogative, and now for Laws;
Effects unhappy! from a Noble Cause.   160
  Time was, a sober Englishman would knock
His servants up, and rise by five o'clock,
Instruct his Family in every rule,
And send his Wife to Church, his Son to school.

144 Newmarket the race-course *146 romance* fiction *149 Lely* painter to Charles
II *153* 'The Siege of Rhodes by Sir William Davenant, the first opera sung in
England' (Pope). *154 eunuch* see p. 156

To worship like his Fathers was his care;   165
To teach their frugal Virtues to his Heir:
To prove, that Luxury could never hold;
And place, on good Security, his Gold.
Now Times are changed, and one Poetic Itch
Has seized the Court and City, Poor and Rich: 170
Sons, Sires, and Grandsires, all will wear the Bays,
Our Wives read Milton, and our Daughters Plays,
To Theatres, and to Rehearsals throng,
And all our Grace at Table is a Song.
I, who so oft renounce the Muses, lie,   175
Not ——'s self e'er tells more *Fibs* than I;
When, sick of Muse, our follies we deplore,
And promise our best Friends to rhyme no more;
We wake next morning in a raging Fit
And call for Pen and Ink to show our Wit.   180

   He served a 'Prenticeship, who sets up shop;
Ward tried on Puppies, and the Poor, his Drop;
E'en Radcliffe's Doctors travel first to France,
Nor dare to practise till they've learned to dance.
Who builds a Bridge that never drove a pile?   185
(Should Ripley venture, all the World would smile)
But those who cannot write, and those who can,
All rhyme, and scrawl, and scribble, to a man.

   Yet Sir, reflect, the mischief is not great;
These Madmen never hurt the Church or State;   190
Sometimes the Folly benefits mankind;
And rarely Av'rice taints the tuneful mind.
Allow him but his Plaything of a Pen,
He ne'er rebels, or plots, like other men:
Flight of Cashiers, or Mobs, he'll never mind;   195
And knows no losses while the Muse is kind.

171 wear the bays win the poet's crown *176* ——*'s self* 'anon', 'the next man',
or possibly Horace *195 cashiers* the cashier of the South Sea Company fled to
France.

To cheat a friend, or ward, he leaves to Peter;
The good man heaps up nothing but mere metre,
Enjoys his garden and his book in quiet;
And then—a perfect Hermit in his Diet. 200
Of little use the Man you may suppose,
Who says in verse what others say in prose;
Yet let me show, a Poet's of some weight,
And (though no soldier) useful to the State.
What will a Child learn sooner than a song? 205
What better teach a Foreigner the tongue?
What's long or short, each accent where to place,
And speak in public with some sort of grace.
I scarce can think him such a worthless thing,
Unless he praise some monster of a King; 210
Or Virtue, or Religion turn to sport,
To please a lewd, or unbelieving Court.
Unhappy Dryden!—in all Charles's days,
Roscommon only boasts unspotted Bays;
And in our own (excuse some Courtly stains) 215
No whiter page than Addison remains.
He, from the taste obscene reclaims our Youth,
And sets the Passions on the side of Truth,
Forms the soft bosom with the gentlest art,
And pours each human Virtue in the heart. 220
Let Ireland tell, how Wit upheld her cause,
Her Trade supported, and supplied her Laws;
And leave on Swift this grateful verse engraved,
'The Rights a Court attacked, a Poet saved.'
Behold the hand that wrought a Nation's cure, 225
Stretched to relieve the Idiot and the Poor,
Proud Vice to brand, or injured Worth adorn,

---

197 Peter Walter* *212* glances at George II's court and at the Queen's reputation for being a 'freethinker' *221–2* refer to Swift's Irish pamphlets *226* Swift was to leave money for this purpose. *227 adorn* lend lustre to

And stretch the Ray to Ages yet unborn.
Not but there are, who merit other palms;
Hopkins and Sternhold glad the heart with Psalms: 230
The Boys and Girls whom Charity maintains,
Impore your help in these pathetic strains:
How could Devotion touch the country pews,
Unless the Gods bestow'd a proper Muse?
Verse cheers their leisure, Verse assists their work,   235
Verse prays for Peace, or sings down Pope and Turk.
The silenced Preacher yields to potent strain,
And feels that grace his prayer besought in vain,
The blessing thrills through all the labouring throng,
And Heaven is won by violence of Song.   240
    Our rural Ancestors, with little blest,
Patient of labour when the end was rest,
Indulged the day that housed their annual grain,
With feasts and offerings, and a thankful strain:
The joy their wives, their sons, and servants share,   245
Ease of their toil, and partners of their care:
The laugh, the jest, attendants on the bowl,
Smoothed every brow, and opened every soul:
With growing years the pleasing Licence grew,
And Taunts alternate innocently flew.   250
But Times corrupt, and Nature, ill-inclined,
Produced the point that left a sting behind;
Till friend with friend, and families at strife,
Triumphant Malice raged through private life.
Who felt the wrong, or feared it, took the alarm,   255
Appealed to Law, and Justice lent her arm.
At length, by wholesome dread of statutes bound,
The Poets learned to please, and not to wound:

---

228 stretch the ray carry the torch; shed light *230 Hopkins and Sternhold* Tudor translators of the Psalms *232 implore your help* for charity and for better psalms, making 'pathetic strains' a pun *236 Pope and Turk* quoting Hopkins's final prayer, which Pope read as a joke on himself

Most warped to Flattery's side; but some, more nice,
Preserved the freedom, and forbore the vice.   260
Hence Satire rose, that just the medium hit,
And heals with Morals what it hurts with Wit.

We conquered France, but felt our captive's charms;
Her Arts victorious triumphed o'er our Arms:
Britain to soft refinements less a foe,   265
Wit grew polite, and Numbers learned to flow.
Waller was smooth; but Dryden taught to join
The varying verse, the full-resounding line,
The long majestic march, and energy divine.
Though still some traces of our rustic vein   270
And splayfoot verse, remained, and will remain.
Late, very late, correctness grew our care,
When the tired nation breathed from civil war.
Exact Racine, and Corneille's noble fire,
Showed us that France had something to admire.   275
Not but the Tragic spirit was our own,
And full in Shakespeare, fair in Otway shone:
But Otway failed to polish or refine,
And fluent Shakespeare scarce effaced a line.
Even copious Dryden wanted, or forgot,   280
The last and greatest Art, the Art to blot.

Some doubt, if equal pains, or equal fire,
The humbler Muse of comedy require.
But in known Images of life, I guess
The labour greater, as the Indulgence less.   285
Observe how seldom even the best succeed:
Tell me if Congreve's Fools are Fools indeed?
What pert low Dialogue has Farquhar writ!
How Van wants grace, who never wanted wit!

267–9 a triplet, in imitation of Dryden 279 Shakespeare's Folio editors said he
never blotted a line; Jonson retorted 'would he had blotted a thousand'. 284 i.e.
images of life as we know it to be 285 indulgence i.e. of fancy 287 Congreve's fools
were thought too witty to be convincing 288 pert inaptly smart 289 Van Vanbrugh*

The stage how loosely does Astræa tread,   290
Who fairly puts all Characters to bed:
And idle Cibber, how he breaks the laws,
To make poor Pinky eat with vast applause!
But fill their purse, our Poet's work is done,
Alike to them, by Pathos or by Pun.   295
    O you! whom Vanity's light bark conveys
On Fame's mad voyage by the wind of Praise,
With what a shifting gale your course you ply,
For ever sunk too low, or borne too high!
Who pants for glory finds but short repose,   300
A breath revives him, or a breath o'erthrows.
Farewell the stage! if just as thrives the Play,
The silly bard grows fat, or falls away.
    There still remains, to mortify a Wit,
The many-headed Monster of the Pit;   305
A senseless, worthless, and unhonoured crowd;
Who, to disturb their betters mighty proud,
Clattering their sticks before ten lines are spoke,
Call for the Farce, the Bear, or the Black-joke.
What dear delight to Britons Farce affords!   310
Ever the taste of Mobs, but now of Lords
(For Taste, eternal wanderer, now flies
From heads to ears, and now from ears to eyes).
The Play stands still; damn action and discourse,
Back fly the scenes, and enter foot and horse;   315
Pageants on pageants, in long order drawn,
Peers, Heralds, Bishops, Ermine, Gold and Lawn;
The Champion, too! and to complete the jest,
Old Edward's Armour beams on Cibber's breast.

---

290 Astraea name assumed by Aphra Behn *293 Pinky* Penkethman, who in one play ate two chickens 'in three seconds' *301 breath revives* i.e. a puff, favourable notice *breath o'erthrows* a hiss, bad reception *305 pit* a pun *309 Black-joke* popular ballad air *313* i.e. from plays to operas to pantomimes *315 scenes* painted flats *319 armour* borrowed from the tower and worn by Cibber in *Henry VIII*

With laughter sure Democritus had died, 320
Had he beheld an Audience gape so wide.
Let Bear or Elephant be e'er so white,
The people, sure, the people are the sight!
Ah, luckless Poet! stretch thy lungs and roar,
That Bear or Elephant shall heed thee more; 325
While all its throats the Gallery extends,
And all the Thunder of the Pit ascends!
Loud as the Wolves on Orcas' stormy steep,
Howl to the roarings of the Northern deep.
Such is the shout, the long-applauding note, 330
At Quin's high plume, or Oldfield's petticoat;
Or when from Court a birthday suit bestowed,
Sinks the lost Actor in the tawdry load.
Booth enters—hark! the Universal Peal!
'But has he spoken?' Not a syllable. 335
What shook the stage, and made the people stare?
Cato's long wig, flowered gown, and lacquered chair.
    Yet lest you think I rally more than teach,
Or praise malignly Arts I cannot reach,
Let me for once presume t'instruct the times, 340
To know the Poet from the Man of Rhymes:
'Tis He who gives my breast a thousand pains,
Can make me feel each Passion that he feigns;
Enrage, compose, with more than magic Art,
With pity, and with Terror, tear my heart; 345
And snatch me, o'er the earth, or through the air,
To Thebes, to Athens, when he will, and where.
    But not this part of the poetic state
Alone, deserves the favour of the Great:

320 *Democritus* said by Juvenal to be always laughing at the follies of mankind
338 *Orcas* the Orkneys 331 *plume* worn by Quin as Coriolanus *Oldfield* acted
in a play partly written by Pope; she had to hide her stage lover under her petticoat
332 *birthday suit* worn at Royal Birthday celebrations 337 *Cato* in Addison's
play

Think of those Authors, Sir, who would rely   350
More on a Reader's sense, than Gazer's eye.
Or who shall wander where the Muses sing?
Who climb their Mountain, or who taste their spring?
How shall we fill a Library with Wit,
When Merlin's Cave is half unfurnished yet?   355
    My Liege! why Writers little claim your thought
I guess; and, with their leave, will tell the fault:
We Poets are (upon a Poet's word)
Of all mankind, the creatures most absurd:
The season, when to come, and when to go,   360
To sing, or cease to sing, we never know;
And if we will recite nine hours in ten,
You lose your patience just like other men.
Then, too, we hurt ourselves, when to defend
A single verse, we quarrel with a friend;   365
Repeat unasked; lament, the Wit's too fine
For vulgar eyes, and point out every line.
But most, when straining with too weak a wing,
We needs will write Epistles to the King;
And from the moment we oblige the town,   370
Expect a Place, or Pension from the Crown;
Or dubbed Historians by express command,
To enrol your triumphs o'er the seas and land,
Be call'd to Court, to plan some work divine,
As once for LOUIS, Boileau and Racine.   375
    Yet think, great Sir! (so many Virtues shown)
Ah think, what Poet best may make them known?
Or choose (at least) some Minister of Grace,
Fit to bestow the Laureate's weighty place.

---

355 Merlin's Cave a quaint building in Richmond Gardens, housing a small but
choice library; contrasted here with the Palatine Library of Horace's Augustus
372 dubbed Historians Dryden and Shadwell were made Historiographers Royal.
375 Boileau and Racine made historiographers to Louis XIV

Charles, to late times to be transmitted fair,   380
Assign'd his figure to Bernini's care;
And great Nassau to Kneller's hand decreed
To fix him graceful on the bounding Steed;
So well in paint and stone they judged of merit;
But Kings in Wit may want discerning spirit.   385
The Hero William, and the Martyr Charles,
One knighted Blackmore, and one pension'd Quarles;
Which made old Ben and surly Dennis swear,
'No Lord's anointed, but a Russian bear.'
    Not with such Majesty, such bold relief,   390
The Forms august of King, or conquering Chief,
E'er swelled on Marble, as in Verse have shined
(In polished Verse) the Manners and the Mind.
Oh! could I mount on the Mæonian wing,
Your Arms, your Actions, your Repose to sing!   395
What seas you traversed, and what fields you fought!
Your Country's Peace, how oft, how dearly bought!
How barb'rous rage subsided at your word,
And Nations wondered, while they dropped the sword!
How, when you nodded, o'er the land and deep,   400
Peace stole her wing, and wrapped the world in sleep;
Till Earth's extremes your mediation own,
And Asia's Tyrants tremble at your Throne.
But Verse, alas! your Majesty disdains;
And I'm not used to Panegyric strains: 405
The Zeal of Fools offends at any time,
But most of all, the Zeal of Fools in rhyme.
Besides, a fate attends on all I write,
That when I aim at praise, they say I bite.

381 Bernini great architect and sculptor; he made a bust of Charles I. *382 Kneller*
painted the William III portrait now at Hampton Court *387–9* the poet Blackmore
was in fact knighted as court physician; nothing is known of Quarles, the emblem
poet, getting a pension; the jeers of Jonson and Dennis remain unexplained. *394
Mæonian* Homer was thought to have lived in Maeonia.

A vile Encomium doubly ridicules: 410
There's nothing blackens like the ink of fools;
If true, a woeful likeness; and if lies,
'Praise undeserved is scandal in disguise':
Well may he blush who gives it, or receives;
And when I flatter, let my dirty leaves   415
(Like Journals, Odes, and such forgotten things
As Eusden, Philips, Settle, writ of Kings)
Clothe spice, line trunks, or flutt'ring in a row,
Befringe the rails of Bedlam and Soho.

Epilogue to the Satires

The two dialogues that compose the Epilogue to the *Satires* were published in 1738. They are not modelled on specific Horatian poems (although the first opens like Satire II 3) but they are astringent extensions of the method used already in the imitation that Pope had addressed to Fortescue (Satire II 1).

The attitude of the Friend in the earlier poem—diplomatic, circumspect, and legalistic—is here extravagantly caricatured; caution and temperance are now associated with a craven disposition to acquiesce in folly and injustice:

> To Vice and Folly to confine the jest,
> Sets half the World, God knows, against the rest;
> Did not the Sneer of more impartial men
> At Sense and Virtue balance all again.
> Judicious Wits spread wide the Ridicule,
> And charitably comfort Knave and Fool.

The Poet's role in the Dialogue is to refuse the solace of the Judicious Wit, solicitous only for his own safety. In the poem's

419 Befringe the rails i.e. like broadsheets displayed on railings and offered for sale

final, pageant-like vision, Vice is acclaimed, as all the driving energies of man are subdued to avarice. It is Pope's most resonant indictment of wealth.

The second Dialogue is conspicuously concerned with the proper objects of satire, and with the Poet's response to the wary Friend's counsel, 'Spare then the Person, and expose the Vice'. Pope in private life, as well as under his public mask, saw himself as the scourge of fools and knaves. At the time of writing the Epistle to Arbuthnot, his private letters to Arbuthnot show the same preoccupations and make a similar response to similar advice; in August 1734 he wrote:

I thank you dear Sir for making That your Request to me which I make my Pride, nay my Duty; 'that I should continue my Disdain and abhorrence of Vice, and manifest it still in my writings'. I would indeed do it with more restrictions, and less personally; it is more agreeable to my nature, which those who know it not are greatly mistaken in: But General Satire in Times of General Vice has no force, and is no Punishment: People have ceas'd to be ashamed of it when so many are joind with them; and tis only by hunting One or two from the Herd that any Examples can be made. If a man writ all his Life against the Collective Body of the Banditti, or against Lawyers, would it do the least Good, or lessen the Body? But if some are hung up, or pilloryed, it may prevent others. And in my low Station, with no other Power than this, I hope to deter, if not to reform.

Yet in this most virulent of Pope's works, the presence of the epic and of the lyric poet continues to be felt. The severities of judgement are vindicated by the fidelity of the writing to the strictest laws of its formal being:

> Truth guards the Poet, sanctifies the line,
> And makes Immortal, Verse as mean as mine.

The typography of the first edition is highly elaborate and has been simplified here.

EPILOGUE TO THE SATIRES

ONE THOUSAND SEVEN HUNDRED AND THIRTY-EIGHT

DIALOGUE I

Friend. NOT twice a twelvemonth you appear in print,
And when it comes, the Court see nothing in 't.
You grow *correct*, that once with Rapture writ,
And are, besides, too *moral* for a Wit.
Decay of Parts, alas! we all must feel—   5
Why now, this moment, don't I see you steal?
'Tis all from *Horace*; *Horace* long before ye
Said, 'Tories call'd him Whig, and Whigs a Tory';
And taught his Romans, in much better metre,
'To laugh at Fools who put their trust in *Peter.*'   10
    But *Horace*, Sir, was delicate, was nice;
Bubo observes, he lashed no sort of *Vice*:
Horace would say, Sir Billy *served the Crown,*
Blunt *could do Business*, H–ggins *knew the Town*;
In Sappho touch the *Failings of the Sex,*   15
In reverend Bishops note some *small Neglects,*
And own the Spaniard did a *waggish thing.*
Who cropped our ears, and sent them to the King.
His sly, polite, insinuating style
Could please at Court, and make AUGUSTUS smile: 20
An artful Manager, that crept between

---

7 from Horace the poem opens like Horace's Satire II iii. *8, 10* Pope quotes himself, see pp. 141, 142. *12 Bubo* Dodington* *Billy* Yonge* *14 H–ggins* Huggins, a corrupt jailer of the Fleet prison *15 Sappho* Lady Montagu* *17 Spaniard* the captain who occasioned the War of Jenkins' Ear, to the delight of the war party *20 Augustus* George II *21 Manager* parliamentary official managing affairs 'between' Lords and Commons; here alluding perhaps to Walpole who 'screened' from the King the scandals of his reign

His Friend and Shame, and was a kind of *Screen.*
But 'faith your very Friends will soon be sore;
Patriots there are, who wish you'd jest no more—
And where's the Glory? 'twill be only thought   25
The Great man never offer'd you a Groat.
Go see Sir ROBERT!—

            P. See Sir ROBERT!—hum—
And never laugh—for all my life to come?
Seen him I have, but in his happier hour
Of Social Pleasure, ill-exchanged for Power;   30
Seen him, uncumbered with the Venal tribe,
Smile without Art, and win without a Bribe.
Would he oblige me? let me only find,
He does not think me what he thinks mankind.
Come, come, at all I laugh he laughs, no doubt;   35
The only difference is, I dare laugh out.

    F. Why, yes: with *Scripture* still you may be free;
A horse-laugh, if you please, at *Honesty;*
A joke on Jekyl, or some odd *Old Whig*
Who never changed his Principle, or Wig;   40
A Patriot is a Fool in every age,
Whom all Lord Chamberlains allow the Stage:
These nothing hurts; they keep their Fashion still,
And wear their strange old Virtue, as they will.

    If any ask you, 'Who's the man, so near   45
His Prince, that writes in verse, and has his ear?'
Why answer, Lyttleton, and I'll engage
The worthy youth shall ne'er be in a rage:
But were his verses vile, his whisper base,
You'd quickly find him in Lord Fanny's case.

---

24 Patriots Opposition members *26 great man* prime minister *39 Jekyl* a great
Whig of the old school *40 wig* i.e. Jekyl still wore the old full-bottomed sort
42 Chamberlains Walpole restored political censorship to the theatre. *48 in a rage*
i.e. at Pope's satire *50 Fanny* Hervey*

Sejanus, Wolsey, hurt not honest Fleury,
But well may put some Statesmen in a fury.

    Laugh then at any, but at Fools or Foes;
These you but anger, and you mend not those.
Laugh at your Friends, and, if your Friends are sore,   55
So much the better, you may laugh the more.
To Vice and Folly to confine the jest,
Sets half the World, God knows, against the rest;
Did not the Sneer of more impartial men
At Sense and Virtue balance all again.   60
Judicious Wits spread wide the Ridicule,
And charitably comfort Knave and Fool.

    P. Dear Sir, forgive the Prejudice of Youth:
Adieu Distinction, Satire, Warmth, and Truth!
Come, harmless *Characters*, that no one hit;   65
Come, Henley's oratory, Osborne's wit!
The Honey dropping from Favonio's tongue,
The Flowers of Bubo, and the Flow of Y—ng!
The gracious Dew of Pulpit Eloquence,
And all the well-whipt Cream of Courtly Sense,   70
That first was H—vy's, F—'s next, and then
The S—te's, and then H—vy's once again.
O come, that easy, Ciceronian style,
So Latin, yet so English all the while,
As, though the pride of Middleton and Bland,   75
All Boys may read, and Girls may understand!
Then might I sing, without the least offence,
And all I sung should be the Nation's Sense;

---

51 *Sejanus* a cruel Roman minister *Wolsey* traitorous minister to Henry VIII
59 *impartial* here, 'indifferent to right and wrong' 65 *harmless Characters* humorous character-sketches in the manner of Theophrastus 67 *Favonio* name for spring breeze—'any gentle poet' 68 *Y—ng* Yonge* 70–2 allude to a formal address of condolence on the Queen's death; Pope says Hervey wrote it, Henry Fox delivered it to Parliament (the Senate) and then Hervey made a Latin epitaph of it.
75 *Middleton and Bland* classical scholars 78 *Nation's sense* official opinion

Or teach the melancholy Muse to mourn,
Hang the sad Verse on CAROLINA's Urn,   80
And hail her passage to the Realms of Rest,
All Parts performed, and *all* her Children blessed!
So—Satire is no more—I feel it die—
No Gazetteer more innocent than I—
And let, a-God's name, every Fool and Knave   85
Be graced through Life, and flattered in his Grave.
    F. Why so? if Satire knows its Time and Place,
You still may lash the Greatest—in disgrace:
For Merit will by turns forsake them all;
Would you know when ? exactly when they fall.   90
But let all Satire in all Changes spare
Immortal S—k, and grave De—re.
Silent and soft, as Saints removed to Heaven,
All Ties dissolved, and every Sin forgiven,
These, may some gentle, ministerial Wing   95
Receive, and place for ever near a King!
There, where no Passion, Pride, or Shame transport,
Lulled with the sweet Nepenthe of a Court,
There, where no Father's, Brother's, Friend's Disgrace
Once break their Rest, or stir them from their Place: 100
But past the Sense of human Miseries,
All Tears are wiped for ever from all Eyes;
No Cheek is known to blush, no Heart to throb,
Save when they lose a Question, or a Job.
    P. Good Heaven forbid, that I should blast their Glory,
Who know how like Whig—ministers to Tory,   [105
And when three Sovereigns died, could scarce be vexed,
Considering what a Gracious Prince was next.

82 the Queen did not receive the last rites and was said not to have blessed the
Prince of Wales *84 gazetteer* official reporter *89 merit* i.e. in official eyes *92 S—k*
Selkirk, Douglas* *De—re* De la Warr, West* *95 ministerial wing* ministering
angel; government party *98 Nepenthe* a sedative *102* from Isaiah xxv 8 *104 lose
a question* are defeated in Parliament *108 Prince* either George II or the Prince
of Wales who opposed him

Have I in silent wonder seen such things
As Pride in Slaves, and Avarice in Kings;   110
And at a Peer, or Peeress, shall I fret,
Who starves a Sister, or forswears a Debt?
Virtue, I grant you, is an empty boast;
But shall the Dignity of *Vice* be lost?
Ye Gods! shall Cibber's son, without rebuke,   115
Swear like a Lord, or a Rich outwhore a Duke?
A fav'rite's Porter with his Master vie,
Be bribed as often, and as often lie?
Shall Ward draw Contracts with a Statesman's skill?
Or Japhet pocket, like his Grace, a Will?   120
Is it for Bond, or Peter (paltry things),
To pay their Debts or keep their Faith like Kings?
If Blount dispatched himself, he played the man,
And so may'st thou, illustrious Passeran!
But shall a Printer, weary of his life,   125
Learn from their Books to hang himself and Wife?
This, this, my friend, I cannot, must not bear;
Vice thus abused, demands a Nation's care;
This calls the Church to deprecate our Sin,
And hurls the Thunder of the Laws on *Gin*.   130
      Let modest Foster, if he will, excel
Ten Metropolitans in preaching well;
A simple Quaker, or a Quaker's wife,
Outdo Landaff, in Doctrine,—yea, in Life:

---

111 Peeress Lady Montagu* *113 empty boast* pride of the starving or brag of the
rest *116 Rich* an actor-manager *120 Japhet* Crook* *his Grace* Prince Frederick
suppressed George I's will *121 Peter* Walter* *123 Blount* a deist; he killed
himself through pretending suicide when his love was rejected *124 Passeran*
another 'freethinker'; he wrote a book on death *125 Printer* Richard Smith, who
hanged himself and his wife and left a letter blaming the freethinkers *129* i.e. the
Church deprecates the spread of sin to the lower ranks *130 gin* its consumption
was restrained by Parliament in 1736 *131 Foster* Anabaptist minister *132 Metropolitans* 'archbishops' *134 Landaff* John Harris; 'A poor bishopric in Wales, as
poorly supplied' (Pope)

Let humble Allen, with an awkward Shame,   135
Do good by stealth, and blush to find it Fame.
Virtue may choose the high or low Degree,
'Tis just alike to Virtue, and to me;
Dwell in a Monk, or light upon a King,
She's still the same, beloved, contented thing.   140
Vice is undone, if she forgets her Birth,
And stoops from Angels to the Dregs of Earth:
But 'tis the Fall degrades her to a Whore;
Let Greatness own her, and she's mean no more:
Her Birth, her Beauty, Crowds and Courts confess,   145
Chaste Matrons praise her, and grave Bishops bless;
In golden Chains the willing World she draws,
And hers the Gospel is, and hers the Laws,
Mounts the Tribunal, lifts her scarlet head,
And sees pale Virtue carted in her stead.   150
Lo! at the Wheels of her Triumphal Car,
Old England's Genius, rough with many a Scar,
Dragged in the Dust! his Arms hang idly round,
His flag inverted trails along the ground!
Our Youth, all liveried o'er with foreign Gold,   155
Before her dance; behind her, crawl the Old!
See thronging Millions to the Pagod run,
And offer Country, Parent, Wife, or Son!
Hear her black Trumpet through the Land proclaim,
That 'Not to be corrupted is the Shame!'   160
In Soldier, Churchman, Patriot, Man in Power,
'Tis Avarice all, Ambition is no more!
See, all our Nobles begging to be Slaves!
See, all our Fools aspiring to be Knaves!
The Wit of Cheats, the Courage of a Whore,   165
Are what ten thousand envy and adore:

141 her birth both in high society and among the rebel angels *149 scarlet* like the
whore of Revelations xvii *157 Pagod* golden coin, oriental temple or idol; here,
the Whore

All, all look up, with reverential Awe,
At Crimes that 'scape, or triumph o'er the Law:
While Truth, Worth, Wisdom, daily they decry—
'Nothing is Sacred now but Villainy.'   170

Yet may this Verse (if such a Verse remain)
Show there was one who held it in disdain.

ONE THOUSAND SEVEN HUNDRED AND THIRTY-EIGHT

DIALOGUE II

Friend. 'Tis all a Libel—Paxton (sir) will say.
  P. Not yet, my Friend! to-morrow, 'faith, it may;
And for that very cause I print to-day.
How should I fret to mangle every line,
In reverence to the Sins of *Thirty-nine*!   5
Vice with such Giant strides comes on amain,
Invention strives to be before in vain;
Feign what I will, and paint it e'er so strong,
Some rising Genius sins up to my Song.
  F. Yet none but you by Name the Guilty lash;   10
E'en Guthrie saves half Newgate by a Dash.
Spare then the Person, and expose the Vice.
  P. How, Sir! not damn the Sharper, but the Dice?
Come on then Satire! general, unconfined,
Spread thy broad wing, and souse on all the Kind.   15
Ye Statesmen, Priests, of one Religion all!
Ye Tradesmen vile, in Army, Court, or Hall!

1 Paxton employed under Walpole to report libels on the government *11 Guthrie*
Newgate chaplain who printed extorted confessions, often under initials only *15
souse* swoop like a hawk *16 one religion* i.e. of Mammon *17 hall* market-hall or
Westminster

Ye Reverend Atheists. *F.* Scandal! name them, Who?
   P. Why that's the thing you bid me not to do.
Who starved a Sister, who forswore a Debt,   20
I never named; the town's inquiring yet.
The poisoning dame— *F.* You mean— *P.* I don't— *F.* You do.
   P. See, now I keep the Secret, and not you.
The bribing Statesman— *F.* Hold! too high you go.
   P. The bribed Elector— *F.* There you stoop too low.   25
   P. I fain would please you, if I knew with what;
Tell me, which Knave is lawful Game, which not?
Must great Offenders, once escaped the Crown,
Like Royal Harts, be never more run down?
Admit your Law to spare the Knight requires?   30
As Beasts of Nature may we hunt the Squires?
Suppose I censure—you know what I mean—
To save a Bishop, may I name a Dean?
   F. A Dean, Sir? no: his Fortune is not made,
You hurt a man that's rising in the Trade.   35
   P. If not the Tradesman who set up to-day,
Much less the 'Prentice who to-morrow may.
Down, down, proud Satire! though a Realm be spoiled,
Arraign no mightier Thief than wretched Wild;
Or, if a Court or Country's made a Job,   40
Go drench a Pickpocket, and join the Mob.
   But Sir, I beg you for the Love of Vice!,
The matter's weighty, pray consider twice:
Have you less Pity for the needy Cheat,
The poor and friendless Villain, than the Great?   45
Alas! the small Discredit of a Bribe
Scarce hurts the Lawyer, but undoes the Scribe.
Then better sure it Charity becomes
To tax Directors, who (thank God) have Plums;

21–2 see pp. 143, 180 *32* meaning the 'reverend atheists' *39 Wild* Jonathan Wild, a thief often likened to Walpole, as later in Fielding's novel *47 scribe* clerk *49 tax* a pun *plum* £100,000

Still better, Ministers; or, if the thing   50
May pinch e'en there—why lay it on a King.
    F. Stop! stop!
                P. Must Satire, then, nor *rise* nor *fall?*
Speak out, and bid me blame no Rogues at all.
    F. Yes, strike that Wild, I'll justify the blow.
    P. Strike? why the man was hanged ten years ago: 55
Who now that obsolete Example fears?
E'en Peter trembles only for his Ears.
    F. What, always Peter? Peter thinks you mad,
You make men desperate if they once are bad:
Else might he take to Virtue some years hence—   60
    P. As S——k, if he lives, will love the Prince.
    F. Strange spleen to S——k!
                    P. Do I wrong the Man?
God knows, I praise a Courtier where I can.
When I confess there *is* who feels for Fame,
And melts to Goodness, need I Scarborough name?   65
Pleased, let me own, in Esher's peaceful Grove
(Where Kent and Nature vie for Pelham's Love),
The Scene, the Master, opening to my view;
I sit and dream I see my Craggs anew!
    Even in a Bishop I can spy Desert;   70
Secker is decent, Rundle has a Heart.
Manners with Candour are to Benson given,
To Berkeley, ev'ry Virtue under Heaven.
    But does the Court a worthy Man remove?
That instant, I declare, he has my Love: 75
I shun his Zenith, court his mild Decline;
Thus Somers once, and Halifax, were mine.

---

57 Peter Walter* *S—k* Selkirk, Douglas* *61 if he lives* i.e. if the Prince prospers
and inherits the throne *66 own* confess *Esher* Pelham's estate *67 Kent* William
Kent, the landscape gardener *68 master* perhaps in the sense 'masterpiece' *71
decent* seemly, temperate *76–83* the opening metaphor is sustained throughout.

Oft in the clear, still Mirror of Retreat,
I studied Shrewsbury, the wise and great:
Carleton's calm Sense, and Stanhope's noble Flame,   80
Compared, and knew their generous End the same:
How pleasing Atterbury's softer hour!
How shined the Soul, unconquered in the Tower!
How can I Pulteney, Chesterfield, forget
While Roman spirit charms; and Attic wit: 85
Argyll, the State's whole Thunder born to wield,
And shake alike the Senate and the Field?
Or Wyndham, just to Freedom and the Throne,
The Master of our Passions, and his own?
Names, which I long have loved, nor loved in vain,   90
Ranked with their Friends, not numbered with their Train;
And, if yet higher the proud List should end,
Still let me say,—No Follower, but a Friend.

    Yet think not Friendship only prompts my Lays;
I follow *Virtue*; where she shines, I praise: 95
Point she to Priest or Elder, Whig or Tory,
Or round a Quaker's Beaver cast a Glory.
I never (to my sorrow I declare)
Dined with the Man of Ross, or my Lord Mayor.
Some, in their choice of Friends (nay, look not grave),   100
Have still a secret Bias to a Knave:
To find an honest man I beat about,
And love him, court him, praise him, in or out.
    F. Then why so few commended?

                        P. Not so fierce;
Find you the Virtue, and I'll find the Verse.   105
But random Praise—the Task can ne'er be done:
Each Mother asks it for her Booby Son,

---

81 generous noble *85 Roman spirit* i.e. of Pulteney's speeches *Attic wit* i.e. the
Athenian eloquence of Lord Chesterfield *92 yet higher* alluding to Pope's friendship with the Prince of Wales *96 elder* officer of the Presbyterian Church *97
beaver* felt hat *glory* halo *99 Man of Ross* Kyrle* *Lord Mayor* Barnard*

Each Widow asks it for the Best of Men,
For him she weeps, and him she weds again.
Praise cannot stoop, like Satire, to the Ground: 110
The Number may be hanged, but not be crowned.
Enough for half the Greatest of these days
To 'scape my Censure, not expect my Praise.
Are they not rich? what more can they pretend?
Dare they to hope a Poet for their Friend?   115
What Richelieu wanted, Louis scarce could gain,
And what young Ammon wished, but wished in vain.
No Power the Muse's Friendship can command;
No Power, when Virtue claims it, can withstand:
To *Cato*, *Virgil* paid one honest line;   120
O let my Country's Friends illumine mine!
—What are you thinking?

                    F. Faith, the thought's no sin:
I think your Friends are out, and would be in.
    P. If merely to come in, Sir, they go out,
The way they take is strangely round about.   125
    F. They too may be corrupted, you'll allow?
    P. I only call those Knaves who are so now.
Is that too little? Come then, I'll comply—
Spirit of Arnall! aid me while I lie.
Cobham's a Coward, Polwarth is a Slave,   130
And Lyttleton a dark, designing Knave;
St John has ever been a wealthy Fool—
But, let me add, Sir Robert's might dull,
Has never made a Friend in private life,
And was, besides, a Tyrant to his Wife.   135

108 widow one who asked Pope for an epitaph on her husband *110 stoop* like
a falcon *111 number* populace *114 pretend* aspire to *116 wanted* lacked *Louis* i.e.
Louis XIV, scarcely honoured by Boileau's flatteries *117 young Ammon* Alexander
the Great, who envied Achilles his poet, Homer *120 honest line Aeneid* viii 670,
commending the justness of Cato of Utica, republican opponent of Caesar

But pray, when others praise him, do I blame?
Call Verres, Wolsey, any odious name?
Why rail they then, if but a Wreath of mine,
Oh All-accomplished St John! deck thy Shrine?
    What! shall each spur-galled Hackney of the Day,   140
When Paxton gives him double Pots and Pay,
Or each new-pensioned Sycophant, pretend
To break my Windows, if I treat a Friend;
Then wisely plead, to me they meant no hurt,
But 'twas my Guest at whom they threw the dirt?   145
Sure, if I spare the Minister, no rules
Of Honour bind me, not to maul his Tools;
Sure, if they cannot cut, it may be said
His Saws are toothless, and his Hatchets Lead.
    It angered Turenne, once upon a day,   150
To see a Footman kicked that took his pay;
But when he heard the Affront the Fellow gave,
Knew one a Man of Honour, one a Knave;
The prudent Gen'ral turned it to a jest,
And begged he'd take the pains to kick the rest: 155
Which not at present having time to do—
    F. Hold Sir! for God's sake, where's the Affront to you?
Against your worship when had S——k writ?
Or P—ge poured forth the Torrent of his Wit?
Or grant, the Bard whose Distich all commend   160
('In Power a Servant, out of Power a Friend')
To W——le guilty of some venial sin;
What's that to you who ne'er was out nor in?
    The Priest whose Flattery bedropped the Crown,
How hurt he you? he only stained the Gown.   165

---

137 Verres a cruel Sicilian ruler impeached by Cicero *138 rail they* a Government newspaper attacked Pope for praising Bolingbroke. *143 break my windows* once done when Bolingbroke was Pope's guest *150 Turenne* a Marshal of France *153 one a knave* i.e. the footman in Turenne's pay *158 S—k* Douglas* *159 P—ge* Judge Page* *160 bard* Dodington,* quoting his Epistle to Walpole

And how did, pray, the Florid Youth offend,
Whose Speech you took, and gave it to a Friend?
    P. Faith, it imports not much from whom it came;
Whoever borrowed, could not be to blame,
Since the whole House did afterwards the same: 170
Let Courtly Wits to Wits afford supply,
As Hog to Hog in Huts of Westphaly:
If one, through Nature's Bounty or his Lord's,
Has what the frugal, dirty soil affords,
From him the next receives it, thick or thin,   175
As pure a Mess almost as it came in;
The blessed Benefit, not there confined,
Drops to the third who nuzzles close behind:
From tail to mouth, they feed, and they carouse:
The last, full fairly gives it to the House.   180
    F. This filthy Simile, this beastly Line,
Quite turns my Stomach— *P.* So does Flattery mine;
And all your Courtly Civet-Cats can vent,
Perfume to you, to me is Excrement.
But hear me further:—Japhet, 'tis agreed,   185
Writ not, and Chartres scarce could write or read,
In all the courts of Pindus guiltless quite;
But pens can Forge, my Friend, that cannot write:
And must no Egg in Japhet's Face be thrown,
Because the Deed he forged was not my own?   190
Must never Patriot then declaim at Gin,
Unless, good man! he has been fairly in?
No zealous Pastor blame a failing Spouse,
Without a staring Reason on his Brows?

---

166 florid youth Henry Fox; see p. 178 *172 Westphaly* German province noted
for pigs *174 frugal, dirty soil* i.e. the mean and corrupt court *185 Japhet* Crook*
187 Pindus mountain associated with the Muses *190 not my own* i.e. Pope had no
personal grievance against Crook *191 patriot* in usual sense; also 'opposition
supporter' *192 fairly in* gin-sozzled in office *193 failing spouse* erring wife;
impotent husband *194 staring reason* upstanding cuckold's horns

And each Blasphemer quite escape the Rod,   195
Because the insult's not on Man, but God?
   Ask you what Provocation I have had?
The strong Antipathy of Good to Bad.
When Truth or Virtue an Affront endures,
The Affront is mine, my Friend, and should be yours.   200
Mine, as a Foe professed to false Pretence,
Who think a Coxcomb's Honour like his Sense;
Mine, as a Friend to every worthy mind;
And mine as Man, who feel for all mankind.
   F. You're strangely proud.

                        P. So proud, I am no Slave: 205
So impudent, I own myself no Knave:
So odd, my Country's Ruin makes me grave.
Yes, I am proud; I must be proud to see
Men not afraid of God, afraid of me:
Safe from the Bar, the Pulpit, and the Throne,   210
Yet touched and shamed by *Ridicule* alone.
   O sacred Weapon! left for Truth's defence,
Sole Dread of Folly, Vice, and Insolence!
To all but Heaven-directed hands denied,
The Muse may give thee, but the gods must guide: 215
Reverent I touch thee! but with honest zeal;
To rouse the Watchmen of the Public Weal,
To Virtue's Work provoke the tardy Hall,
And goad the Prelate slumbering in his Stall.
   Ye tinsel Insects! whom a Court maintains,   220
That counts your Beauties only by your Stains,
Spin all your Cobwebs o'er the Eye of Day!
The Muse's wing shall brush you all away:

---

202 honour . . . sense i.e. neither can be respected *209 not afraid* without reverence
for *afraid* frightened of *214 Heaven-directed* guided by the gods; supplicating
218 Hall Westminster Hall *219 stall* cathedral seat *221 stains* colours; taints *222
cobwebs* i.e. sophistries *eye of day* the sun; the light of truth

All his Grace preaches, all his Lordship sings,
All that makes Saints of Queens, and Gods of Kings,— 225
All, all but Truth, drops dead-born from the Press,
Like the last Gazette, or the last Address.

When black Ambition stains a Public cause,
A Monarch's sword when mad Vain-glory draws,
Not Waller's wreath can hide the Nation's Scar, 230
Not Boileau turn the Feather to a Star.

Not so, when diademed with Rays divine,
Touched with the Flame that breaks from Virtue's Shrine,
Her Priestless Muse forbids the Good to die,
And opes the Temple of Eternity: 235
There, other Trophies deck the truly Brave,
Than such an Anstis casts into the Grave;
Far other Stars than * and * * wear,
And may descend to Mordington from Stair:
Such as on Hough's unsullied Mitre shine, 240
Or beam, good Digby, from a Heart like thine:
Let Envy howl, while Heaven's whole Chorus sings,
And bark at Honour not conferred by Kings;
Let Flattery sickening see the Incense rise,
Sweet to the World, and grateful to the Skies: 245
Truth guards the Poet, sanctifies the line,
And makes Immortal, Verse as mean as mine.

Yes, the last Pen for Freedom let me draw,
When Truth stands trembling on the edge of Law;
Here, Last of Britons! let your Names be read; 250

---

227 *Gazette* government publication *address* parliamentary response to the King's speech 229 *vain-glory* i.e. the ambition of Cromwell 230 *Waller* twice commemorated Cromwell 231 *Boileau* used the feather-star image in a poem on Louis XIV at Namur. 234 *priestless* i.e. dispensing with last rites 237 *Anstis* the Garter King of Arms 238 * *and* ** George and Frederick, the King and the Prince 239 *Mordington* an obscure lord *Stair* Dalrymple* 240 *Hough* opposed and Digby supported James II's church policy, but Pope regarded both as men of integrity. 249 *edge of law* threatened by censorship: the law's sword-edge; on the brink of anarchy, where all law ends

Are none, none living? let me praise the Dead,
And for that Cause which made your Fathers shine,
Fall by the Votes of their degen'rate Line.

    F. Alas! alas! pray end what you began,
And write next winter more *Essays on Man.*

Three Epitaphs on Two Lovers
Struck Dead by Lightning

THE lovers were killed at harvest-time in the village of Stanton Harcourt, where Pope was staying at the time. According to John Gay, Lord Harcourt doubted if country-people would understand the first version, and Pope wrote the second in a simpler and more pious vein. Perhaps the sentiment of its last lines is less extravagant now than when it was first set down:

> Virtue unmoved can hear the Call,
> And face the Flash that melts the Ball.

The third version might have been done with the assistance of Gay.

THREE EPITAPHS
ON TWO LOVERS STRUCK DEAD
BY LIGHTNING

NEAR THIS PLACE LIE THE BODIES OF
JOHN HEWET AND SARAH DREW
AN INDUSTRIOUS YOUNG MAN, AND
VIRTUOUS MAIDEN OF THIS PARISH;
CONTRACTED IN MARRIAGE
WHO BEING WITH MANY OTHERS AT HARVEST
WORK, WERE BOTH IN AN INSTANT KILLED
BY LIGHTNING ON THE LAST DAY OF JULY
1718

I

WHEN Eastern lovers feed the fun'ral fire,
On the same pile the faithful fair expire:
Here pitying Heaven that virtue mutual found,
And blasted both, that it might neither wound.
Hearts so sincere th' Almighty saw well pleased,   5
Sent his own lightning, and the Victims seized.

II

THINK not by rigorous judgment seized,
    A pair so faithful could expire;
Victims so pure Heaven saw well pleased,
    And snatched them in celestial fire.

Live well and fear no sudden fate;   5
    When God calls Virtue to the grave,
Alike 'tis Justice soon or late,
    Mercy alike to kill or save,

Virtue unmoved can hear the Call,
    And face the Flash that melts the Ball.   10

III

Here lie two poor Lovers, who had the mishap
Though very chaste people, to die of a Clap.

Advertisements
and
Selections

From *SUMMER:*
THE SECOND PASTORAL

See what Delights in Sylvan Scenes appear!
Descending Gods have found Elysium here.   60
In Woods bright Venus with Adonis strayed,
And chaste Diana haunts the Forest Shade.
Come, lovely Nymph, and bless the silent Hours,
When Swains from Shearing seek their nightly Bowers;
When weary Reapers quit the sultry Field,   65
And crowned with Corn, their Thanks to Ceres yield.
This harmless Grove no lurking Viper hides,
But in my Breast the Serpent Love abides.
Here Bees from Blossoms sip the rosy Dew,
But your Alexis knows no Sweets but you.   70
O deign to visit our forsaken Seats,
The mossy Fountains, and the Green Retreats!
Where'er you walk, cool Gales shall fan the Glade,
Trees, where you sit, shall crowd into a Shade:
Where'er you tread, the blushing Flowers shall rise,   75
And all things flourish where you turn your eyes.
Oh, how I long with you to pass my Days,
Invoke the Muses, and resound your praise!
Your Praise the Birds shall chant in every Grove,
And Winds shall waft it to the Powers above.   80
But would you sing, and rival *Orpheus'* Strain,
The wond'ring Forests soon should dance again,
The moving Mountains hear the powerful Call,
And headlong Streams hang list'ning in their Fall.

But see, the Shepherds shun the Noonday Heat,   85
The lowing Herds to murm'ring Brooks retreat,
To closer Shades the panting Flocks remove;
Ye Gods! and is there no Relief for Love?
But soon the Sun with milder Rays descends
To the cool Ocean, where his Journey ends: 90
On me Love's fiercer Flames for ever prey,
By Night he scorches, as he burns by Day.

From *WINDSOR FOREST*

When milder Autumn Summer's Heat succeeds,
And in the new-shorn Field the Partridge feeds,
Before his Lord the ready Spaniel bounds,
Panting with Hope, he tries the furrowed Grounds;   100
But when the tainted Gales the Game betray,
Couched close he lies, and meditates the Prey;
Secure they trust th' unfaithful Field, beset,
Till hov'ring o'er 'em sweeps the swelling Net.
Thus (if small Things we may with great compare)   105
When *Albion* sends her eager Sons to War,
Some thoughtless Town, with Ease and Plenty blest,
Near, and more near, the closing Lines invest;
Sudden they seize th' amazed, defenceless Prize,
And high in Air *Britannia's* Standard flies.   110
See! from the Brake the whirring Pheasant springs,
And mounts exulting on triumphant Wings;
Short is his Joy! he feels the fiery Wound,
Flutters in Blood, and panting beats the Ground.
Ah! what avail his glossy, varying Dyes,   115
His Purple Crest, and Scarlet-circled Eyes,
The vivid Green his shining Plumes unfold,
His painted Wings, and Breast that flames with Gold?

Nor yet, when moist *Arcturus* clouds the Sky
The Woods and Fields their pleasing Toils deny.   120
To Plains with well-breathed Beagles we repair,
And trace the Mazes of the circling Hare.
(Beasts, urged by us, their Fellow Beasts pursue,
And learn of Man each other to undo)
With slaught'ring Guns th' unwearied Fowler roves,   125
When Frosts have whitened all the naked Groves;
Where Doves in Flocks the leafless Trees o'ershade,
And lonely Woodcocks haunt the wat'ry Glade.
He lifts the Tube, and levels with his Eye;
Straight a short Thunder breaks the frozen Sky.   130
Oft, as in Airy Rings they skim the Heath,
The clam'rous Lapwings feel the Leaden Death:
Oft, as the mounting Larks their Notes prepare,
They fall, and leave their little Lives in Air.

In genial Spring, beneath the quiv'ring Shade   135
Where cooling Vapours breathe along the Mead,
The patient Fisher takes his silent Stand
Intent, his Angle trembling in his Hand;
With Looks unmoved, he hopes the Scaly Breed,
And eyes the dancing Cork and bending Reed.   140
Our plenteous Streams a various Race supply,
The bright-eyed Perch with Fins of *Tyrian* Dye,
The silver Eel, in shining Volumes rolled,
The yellow Carp, in Scales bedropped with Gold,
Swift Trouts, diversified with Crimson Stains,   145
And Pikes, the Tyrants of the watery Plains.

.   .   .   .   .

Behold! th' ascending *Villas* on my Side   375
Project long Shadows o'er the Crystal Tide.
Behold! *Augusta's* glitt'ring Spires increase,
And Temples rise, the beauteous Works of Peace.

I see, I see where two fair Cities bend
Their ample Bow, a new *Whitehall* ascend!   380
There mighty Nations shall inquire their Doom,
The World's great Oracle in Times to come;
There Kings shall sue, and suppliant States be seen
Once more to bend before a *British* Queen.

Thy Trees, fair *Windsor*! now shall leave their Woods, 385
And half thy Forests rush into my Floods,
Bear *Britain's* Thunder, and her Cross display,
To the bright Regions of the rising Day;
Tempt Icy Seas, where scarce the Waters roll,
Where clearer Flames glow round the frozen Pole;   390
Or under Southern Skies exalt their Sails,
Led by new Stars, and borne by spicy Gales!
For me the Balm shall bleed, and Amber flow,
The Coral redden, and the Ruby glow,
The Pearly Shell its lucid Globe infold,   395
And *Phœbus* warm the rip'ning *Ore* to *Gold*,
The Time shall come, when free as Seas or Wind
Unbounded *Thames* shall flow for all Mankind,
Whole Nations enter with each swelling Tide,
And Seas but join the Regions they divide;   400
Earth's distant Ends our Glory shall behold,
And the new World launch forth to seek the Old.

From *AN ESSAY ON CRITICISM*

Nature to all things fixed the Limits fit,
And wisely curbed proud Man's pretending Wit.
As on the *Land* while *here* the *Ocean* gains,
In *other Parts* it leaves wide sandy Plains;   55
Thus in the *Soul* while *Memory* prevails,
The solid Power of *Understanding* fails;

Where Beams of warm *Imagination* play,
The *Memory's* soft Figures melt away.
One *Science* only will one *Genius* fit;   60
So *vast* is Art, so *narrow* Human Wit:
Not only bounded to *peculiar Arts*,
But oft in *those*, confined to *single Parts*.
Like Kings we lose the Conquests gained before,
By vain Ambition still to make them more: 65
Each might his *sev'ral Province* well command,
Would all but *stoop* to what they *understand*.
    First follow NATURE, and your Judgment frame
By her just Standard, which is still the same:
Unerring Nature, still divinely bright,   70
One *clear*, *unchanged*, and *Universal* Light,
Life, Force, and Beauty, must to all impart,
At once the *Source*, and *End*, and *Test of Art*.
Art from that Fund each *just Supply* provides;
Works *without Show*, and *without Pomp* presides: 75
In some fair Body thus th' informing Soul
With Spirits feeds, with Vigour fills the whole,
Each Motion guides, and every Nerve sustains;
Itself unseen, but in th' *Effects*, remains.
Some, to whom Heaven in Wit has been profuse,   80
Want as much more, to turn it to its use;
For *Wit* and *Judgment* often are at strife,
Though meant each other's Aid, like *Man* and *Wife*.
'Tis more to *guide* than *spur* the Muse's Steed;
Restrain his Fury, than provoke his Speed;   85
The winged Courser, like a gen'rous Horse,
Shows most true Mettle when you *check* his Course.
    Those RULES of old *discovered*, not *devised*,
Are *Nature* still, but *Nature methodised*:
Nature, like *Liberty*, is but restrained   90
By the same Laws which first *herself* ordained.

     .   .   .   .   .

The gen'rous Critic *fanned* the *Poet's Fire*,   100
And taught the World *with Reason* to *Admire*.
Then Criticism the Muse's Handmaid proved,
To dress her Charms, and make her more belov'd:
But following Wits from that Intention strayed,
Who could not win the Mistress, wooed the Maid;   105
Against the Poets *their own Arms* they turned,
Sure to hate most the Men from whom they *learned*.
So modern '*Pothecaries*, taught the Art
By *Doctor's Bills* to play the *Doctor's Part*,
Bold in the *Practice* of *mistaken Rules*,   110
Prescribe, apply, and call their *Masters* Fools.
Some on the Leaves of ancient Authors prey,
Nor Time nor Moths e'er spoiled so much as they:
Some drily plain, without Invention's Aid,
Write dull *Receipts* how Poems may be made: 115
These leave the Sense, their Learning to display,
And those explain the Meaning quite away.

   You then whose Judgment the right Course would steer,
Know well each ANCIENT's proper *Character*:
His *Fable, Subject, Scope* in every Page;   120
Religion, Country, Genius of his *Age:*
Without all these at once before your Eyes,
Cavil you may, but never *Criticise*.
Be *Homer's* works your *Study*, and *Delight*,
Read them by Day, and meditate by Night;   125
Thence form your Judgment, thence your Maxims bring,
And trace the Muses *upward* to their *Spring*.

      .   .   .   .

   But most by *Numbers* judge a Poet's Song,
And *smooth* or *rough*, with them, is *right* or *wrong*;
In the bright *Muse*, though thousand *Charms* conspire,
Her *Voice* is all these tuneful Fools admire,   340

Who haunt *Parnassus* but to please their Ear,
Not mend their Minds; as some to *Church* repair,
Not for the *Doctrine*, but the *Music* there.
These *Equal Syllables* alone require,
Though oft the Ear the *open Vowels* tire;   345
While *Expletives* their feeble Aid *do* join,
And ten low Words oft creep in one dull Line,
While they ring round the same *unvaried Chimes*,
With sure *Returns* of still *expected Rhymes*;
Wher'er you find *the cooling Western Breeze*,   350
In the next line, it *whispers through the Trees*;
If *Crystal Streams with pleasing Murmurs creep*:
The Reader's threatened (not in vain) with *Sleep*.
Then, at the *last*, and *only* Couplet fraught
With some *unmeaning* Thing they call a *Thought*,   355
A *needless Alexandrine* ends the Song,
That, like a wounded Snake, drags its slow length along.
Leave such to tune their own dull Rhymes, and know
What's *roundly smooth*, or *languishingly slow*;
And praise the *Easy Vigour* of a Line,   360
Where *Denham's* strength, and *Waller's* Sweetness join.
True Ease in Writing comes from Art, not Chance,
As those move easiest who have learned to dance.
'Tis not enough no Harshness give Offence,
The *Sound* must seem an *Echo* to the *Sense*:   365
Soft is the Strain when *Zephyr* gently blows,
And the *smooth Stream* in *smoother Numbers* flows;
But when loud Surges lash the sounding Shore,
The *hoarse, rough Verse* should like the *Torrent* roar.
When *Ajax* strives some Rock's vast Weight to throw,   370
The Line too *labours*, and the Words move *slow*:
Not so, when swift *Camilla* scours the Plain,
Flies o'er the unbending Corn, and skims along the Main.
Hear how *Timotheus'* varied Lays surprise,
And bid Alternate Passions fall and rise!   375

While, at each change, the Son of *Libyan Jove*
Now *burns* with Glory, and then *melts* with Love;
Now his *fierce Eyes* with *sparkling Fury* glow;
Now *Sighs* steal out, and *Tears begin to flow*:
Persians and *Greeks* like *Turns of Nature* found,   380
And the *World's Victor* stood subdued by *Sound*!
The Power of Music all our Hearts allow,
And what *Timotheus* was, is *Dryden* now.

From *AN ESSAY ON MAN*

From Epistle I

The bliss of Man (could Pride that blessing find)
Is not to act or think beyond mankind;   190
No powers of body or of soul to share,
But what his nature and his state can bear.
Why has not Man a microscopic eye?
For this plain reason, Man is not a Fly.
Say what the use, were finer optics given,   195
T' inspect a mite, not comprehend the heaven?
Or touch, if tremblingly alive all o'er,
To smart and agonise at every pore?
Or quick effluvia darting through the brain,
Die of a rose in aromatic pain?   200
If Nature thundered in his opening ears,
And stunned him with the music of the spheres,
How would he wish that Heaven had left him still
The whisp'ring Zephyr, and the purling rill?
Who finds not Providence all good and wise,   205
Alike in what it gives, and what it denies?
Far as Creation's ample range extends,
The scale of sensual, mental powers ascends:

Mark how it mounts to Man's imperial race,
From the green myriads in the peopled grass: 210
What modes of sight betwixt each wide extreme,
The mole's dim curtain, and the lynx's beam:
Of smell, the headlong lioness between,
And hound sagacious on the tainted green:
Of hearing, from the life that fills the flood,   215
To that which warbles through the vernal wood:
The spider's touch, how exquisitely fine!
Feels at each thread, and lives along the line:
In the nice bee, what sense so subtly true
From pois'nous herbs extracts the healing dew: 220
How Instinct varies in the grov'ling swine,
Compared, half-reas'ning elephant, with thine!

From Epistle II

KNOW then thyself, presume not God to scan;
The proper study of Mankind is Man.
Placed on this isthmus of a middle state,
A being darkly wise, and rudely great:
With too much knowledge for the Sceptic side,   5
With too much weakness for the Stoic's pride,
He hangs between; in doubt to act, or rest;
In doubt to deem himself a God, or Beast;
In doubt his Mind or Body to prefer;
Born but to die, and reas'ning but to err;   10
Alike in ignorance, his reason such,
Whether he thinks too little, or too much:
Chaos of Thought and Passion, all confused;
Still by himself abused, or disabused;
Created half to rise, and half to fall;   15
Great lord of all things, yet a prey to all;

Sole judge of Truth, in endless Error hurled:
The glory, jest, and riddle of the world!
  Go, wondrous creature! mount where Science guides,
Go, measure earth, weigh air, and state the tides;   20
Instruct the planets in what orbs to run,
Correct old Time, and regulate the Sun;
Go, soar with Plato to th' empyreal sphere,
To the first good, first perfect, and first fair;
Or tread the mazy round his followers trod,   25
And quitting sense call imitating God;
As Eastern priests in giddy circles run,
And turn their heads to imitate the Sun.
Go, teach Eternal Wisdom how to rule—
Then drop into thyself, and be a fool!   30

From *THE DUNCIAD*

From Book I

  Here she beholds the Chaos dark and deep,   55
Where nameless somethings in their causes sleep,
Till genial Jacob, or a warm Third day,
Call forth each mass, a poem, or a play:
How Hints, like spawn, scarce quick in embryo lie,
How new-born Nonsense first is taught to cry,   60
Maggots half-formed, in rhyme exactly meet,
And learn to crawl upon poetic feet.
Here one poor Word an hundred clenches makes,
And ductile Dulness new meanders takes;
There motley Images her fancy strike,   65
Figures ill-paired, and Similes unlike.
She sees a Mob of Metaphors advance,
Pleased with the Madness of the mazy dance:

How Tragedy and Comedy embrace;
How Farce and Epic get a jumbled race;   70
How Time himself stands still at her command,
Realms shift their place, and Ocean turns to land.
Here gay Description Egypt glads with showers,
Or gives to Zembla fruits, to Barca flowers;
Glitt'ring with ice here hoary hills are seen,   75
There painted valleys of eternal green.
In cold December fragrant chaplets blow,
And heavy harvests nod beneath the snow.

THE DUNCIAD

From Book II

Three College Sophs, and three pert Templars came,
The same their talents, and their tastes the same;   380
Each prompt to query, answer, and debate,
And smit with love of Poesy and Prate.
The pond'rous books two gentle readers bring;
The heroes sit, the vulgar form a ring.
The clam'rous crowd is hushed with mugs of Mum,   385
Till all, tuned equal, send a gen'ral hum.
Then mount the Clerks, and in one lazy tone
Through the long, heavy, painful page drawl on;
Soft creeping, words on words, the sense compose;
At ev'ry line they stretch, they yawn, they doze.   390
As to soft gales top-heavy pines bow low
Their heads, and lift them as they cease to blow:
Thus oft they rear, and oft the head decline,
As breathe, or pause, by fits, the airs divine.
And now to this side, now to that they nod,   395
As verse, or prose, infuse the drowsy God.

Thrice Budgel aimed to speak, but thrice suppressed
By potent Arthur, knocked his chin and breast.
Toland and Tindal, prompt at priests to jeer,
Yet silent bowed to 'Christ's no kingdom here.'　　　　400
Who sate the nearest, by the words o'ercome,
Slept first; the distant nodded to the hum.
Then down are rolled the books; stretched o'er 'em lies
Each gentle clerk, and mutt'ring seals his eyes.
As what a Dutchman plumps into the lakes,　　　　405
One circle first, and then a second makes;
What Dulness dropped among her sons impressed
Like motion from one circle to the rest;
So from the mid-most the nutation spreads
Round and more round, o'er all the sea of heads.　　　　410

THE DUNCIAD

From Book IV

In vain, in vain—the all-composing Hour
Resistless falls: the Muse obeys the Pow'r.
She comes! she comes! the sable Throne behold
Of *Night* Primeval and of *Chaos* old!　　　　630
Before her, *Fancy's* gilded clouds decay,
And all its varying Rainbows die away.
Wit shoots in vain its momentary fires,
The meteor drops, and in a flash expires.
As one by one, at dread Medea's strain,　　　　635
The sick'ning stars fade off th' ethereal plain;
As Argus' eyes by Hermes' wand oppressed,
Closed one by one to everlasting rest;
Thus at her felt approach, and secret might,
Art after *Art* goes out, and all is Night.　　　　640

See skulking *Truth* to her old Cavern fled,
Mountains of Casuistry heaped o'er her head!
Philosophy, that leaned on Heaven before,
Shrinks to her second cause, and is no more.
Physic of *Metaphysic* begs defence,   645
And *Metaphysic* calls for aid on *Sense*!
See *Mystery* to *Mathematics* fly!
In vain! they gaze, turn giddy, rave, and die.
Religion blushing veils her sacred fires,
And unawares *Morality* expires.   650
Nor *public* flame, nor *private*, dares to shine,
Nor *human* Spark is left, nor Glimpse *divine*!
Lo! thy dread Empire, CHAOS! is restored;
Light dies before thy uncreating word:
Thy hand, great Anarch! lets the curtain fall;   655
And Universal Darkness buries All.

Guide to Names

ADDISON, Joseph
Pope admired Addison as the editor of *The Spectator* (see p. 167) but resented his pretences as leader of a literary élite (see p. 130).

ALLEN, Ralph
Assistant postmaster at Bath; philanthropist, and patron of the authorized edition of Pope's letters.

ARNALL, William
A hack government journalist; wrote for *The Free Briton*; mentioned in *Dunciad* II 315.

ATTERBURY, Francis
Bishop of Rochester; imprisoned and banished for his Jacobite allegiances. Friend of Pope and a member of the Scriblerus Club.

BARNARD, Sir John
M.P. for the City of London; Lord Mayor 1737-8; reputation for great public integrity.

BATHURST, Allen, Earl Bathurst
Tory peer and friend of Pope; shared Pope's interest in gardens and asked his advice about the treatment of his own grounds.

BENSON, Martin
Bishop of Gloucester; much admired for his rectitude and learning.

BENTLEY, Richard
Master of Trinity, Cambridge; classical scholar and editor of Milton. Said to have mocked Pope's Homer.

BETHEL, Hugh
M.P. for Pontefract; close friend of Pope, and lover of a quiet, country life.

BLACKMORE, Sir Richard
Court physician and minor epic poet. Quarrelled with Pope about a burlesque version of the first Psalm.

BLUNT, Sir John
Director of the South Sea Company; said by Pope to be a severe critic of the vices of his time.

BOLINGBROKE, Viscount. Henry St John
Leading Tory statesman and philosopher; attainted by George I; leader of opposition party from 1723 to 1735. Bolingbroke's political and philosophical ideas were partly adapted by Pope in his *Essay on Man*.

BOND, Denis
M.P. for Dorchester; expelled from Commons; convicted of embezzlement.

BOYLE, Henry, Baron Carleton.
Bolingbroke's predecessor as Secretary of State (1708–19); President of the Council under Walpole; noted for his modesty and soundness of judgement.

BUCKINGHAM, Duke of. John Sheffield (1648–1721)
Lord Privy Seal, and holder of other high offices in law; poet, and friend of Dryden; wrote verses on Pope for the 1717 poems.

BUCKINGHAM, Duke of. George Villiers (d. 1687)
Pope believed the story that Villiers died in an ale-house at Helmsley. In fact he continued in reasonable prosperity to his death.

BUDGELL, Eustace
Contributor to *The Spectator*; driven to suicide by a sequence of lawsuits.

CARYLL, John
See p. 28.

CHANDOS, Duke of. James Brydges.
Wealthy Whig M.P. and patron of the arts. His mansion at Canons was

of great scale and splendour. Pope calls him 'gracious Chandos' in his Epistle to Cobham, to make up for the offence that some thought intended under the character of Timon (see p. 117).

CHARTRES, Francis
Pimp, profligate and gambler; also a colonel, a Whig and sometime in the service of Walpole; subject of a famous epitaph by Arbuthnot, and possibly depicted in Hogarth's *Harlot's Progress* Plate 1.

CHESELDEN, William
Distinguished surgeon and wit; attended Pope in his last illness.

CIBBER, Colley
Comic playwright and actor. Pope admired his best play, *The Careless Husband*, but quarrelled with him and made him the hero of *The Dunciad*. His son Theophilus took over at Drury Lane.

CLARKE, Samuel
Cambridge philosopher; considered unorthodox; disliked by Bolingbroke and therefore by Pope.

COBHAM, Viscount. Sir Richard Temple,
Leading Whig; joined Walpole opposition; developed the gardens at his family seat at Stowe; friend of Pope.

COLEPEPPER, Sir William
A gambler who ruined himself and lived on, says Pope, 'to see the ruin of others' in the gaming-house.

CONINGSBY, Thomas
Whig politician, partly responsible for the impeachment of Harley.

CROOK, Japhet
Notorious forger; cruelly pilloried, and imprisoned 'for life' in 1731. He died in 1734.

CURLL, Edmund
Disreputable bookseller and publisher; involved in a complicated intrigue with Pope, who tricked him into publishing an unauthorized edition of the letters.

CUTLER, Sir John
A rich London merchant whose private parsimony won him notoriety as a miser, in spite of his many public benefactions.

DALRYMPLE, John, Earl of Stair
Ambassador at Paris; of excellent reputation, but deprived of his post after opposing Walpole's excise bill.

DARNLEY, Katherine, Duchess of Buckinghamshire
An arrogant and quarrelsome woman, engaged in constant law-suits with her own children. F. W. Bateson (Twickenham edition III ii) finds her the original of Atossa.

DODINGTON, George Bubb, Baron Melcombe
Unscrupulous political patron, owning several parliamentary boroughs. He helped Walpole but became adviser to the Prince of Wales. He provoked Pope by identifying 'Timon' with Chandos.

DOUGLAS, Charles, Earl of Selkirk
Representative of Scottish Peers in Parliament; a notorious hanger-on at court.

EUSDEN, Laurence
Parson and poet laureate, with a reputation for drunkenness.

FLEURY, André Hercule de
Adviser to Louis XV; renowed for his judicious and pacific policies.

FOX, Henry
Prominent Whig politician. His brother Stephen was a more obscure M.P. and supporter of Walpole.

GRANVILLE, Earl. John Carteret.
Leading Opposition Whig; assisted in the fall of Walpole and dominated the government as Secretary of State (1742–4).

de GREY, Henry, Duke of Kent
Held several high offices without distinction; said to be reputed for his wealth and for a strong smell that gave him his nickname 'bug'.

GRIMSTON, Lord
Whig M.P.; booby author of a much derided play, *The Lawyer's Fortune, or Love in a Hollow Tree.*

HALES, Stephen
Curate of Teddington and a physiologist who shocked Pope by practising vivisection; witnessed Pope's will.

HALIFAX, Earl of. Charles Montagu.
Sometime Chancellor of the Exchequer; President of the Royal Society; one of Pope's patrons for the translation of *The Iliad*; offered Pope a pension in 1714 but was refused.

HARLEY, Edward, Earl of Oxford.
Great literary patron and librarian; friend of Pope.

HEATHCOTE, Sir Gilbert
A founder of the Bank of England; said to be model for Sir Andrew Freeport in *The Spectator*; unfairly reported a miser.

HENLEY, John
Known as 'Orator Henley'; left the Church and became an independent, itinerant lecturer on 'any branch of knowledge, composition and elocution'. He is possibly portrayed by Hogarth in 'A Midnight Modern Conversation'.

HERVEY, John
Vice-Chamberlain to Walpole and his palace agent with Queen Caroline; took Lady Montagu's part in the quarrel with Pope and ultimately won himself a place in *The Dunciad*.

HOWARD, Henrietta
Possible model for some traits of Chloe in *Moral Essays* II; but she was a close friend of Martha Blount.

HOWARD, Mary, Countess of Delorain
Maid of honour to Queen Caroline, and mistress of George II; said to have tried to poison another maid of honour of whose lover she was jealous.

KYRLE, John
Pope's character of the Man of Ross (p. 106) is a true one, but Kyrle did not in fact found a church or a hospital and he knew little about medicine.

LEE, Nathaniel
Gifted playwright who suffered a mental breakdown and was for some years in Bedlam.

LINTOT, Barnaby Bernard
One of Pope's publishers; after a quarrel over the subscribers to *The Odyssey* Lintot was put in the first *Dunciad*, but in 1735 he was again publishing Pope's *Works*.

LYTTLETON, George
Opposition Whig; secretary to the Prince of Wales; leading opponent of Walpole; a friend of Pope.

MEAD, Richard
Court physician, attended Pope in 1743; a scholar, and friend of Bentley.

MONTAGU, Lady Mary Wortley
Wife of Edward Wortley Montagu; famous for her letters and for her wit; Pope quarrelled with her, perhaps as a result of an early emotional attachment.

MONTAGU, Edward Wortley
M.P. for Huntingdon; held various offices; said to have been rich and self-indulgent; but nevertheless had a reputation for meanness.

OSBORNE, Francis. Pseudonym for James Pitt.
Hack journalist; contributor to *The London Journal* and *The Daily Gazetteer*; figures in *The Dunciad* II 312.

PAGE, Sir Francis
A judge with a (possibly undeserved) reputation for cruelty; Johnson describes his treatment of the poet Savage, convicted of murder, as insolent and severe.

PHILIPS, Ambrose
A pastoral poet whose work was first published with Pope's *Pastoral*; when Philips received the more favourable notice Pope retorted with an ironic review in the *Guardian*. Philips wrote an ode to Walpole. His nickname was 'Namby Pamby'.

POLWARTH, Viscount. Hugh Hume.
Whig opponent of Walpole. His skill and integrity made a deep impression on Walpole and on Pope.

QUEENSBERRY, Duke of. Charles Douglas.
Privy Councillor; quarrelled with George II when a licence was refused for Gay's *Polly*. Gay was a close friend of the family.

RUNDLE, Thomas
Ecclesiastic and theologian; Pope wrote enthusiastically of him in his letters.

SAWYER, Margaret, Countess of Pembroke
A portrait of her, in pastoral style with a lamb, was painted by Jan van der Vaast in about 1687. This and other relevant paintings are at Wilton. Margaret Sawyer's picture is reproduced in the Twickenham edition Vol. III ii.

SETTLE, Elkanah
Poet and playwright; appointed City Poet in 1691; figures in *The Dunciad*.

SMYTHE, James Moore
Son of Arthur Moore (see p. 125); quarrelled with Pope because he retained some Pope verse in one of his comedies after permission had been withdrawn.

SOMERS, John, Baron Somers.
Leading Whig in Queen Anne's reign; encouraged Pope as a poet and befriended him.

TATE, Nahum
Poet and playwright of modest abilities. Adapted *King Lear* to a happy ending.

THEOBALD, Lewis
Poet, playwright and editor of Shakespeare. His attack on Pope's edition (largely justified) won him a leading place in *The Dunciad*.

TOPHAM, Richard
Keeper of the Records in the Tower. Owned a remarkable collection of drawings.

TURENNE, Viscomte de
Marshal of France under Louis XIV. The story Pope tells (p. 187) was published in English in a History of 1735.

VANBRUGH, Sir John
Architect and playwright; see p. 113.

WALPOLE, Sir Robert
Whig Prime Minister 1715–17, 1721–42. Pope struggled to admire the man while denouncing the regime of the politician.

WALTER, Peter
M.P. for Bridport; a 'money scrivener' with a reputation for usury and sharp practice. Swift wrote that he could 'starve twenty lords to make one scoundrel rich'.

WARD, John
M.P. for Weymouth; convicted of forgery and expelled from the Commons in 1726. See p. 98 and p. 180.

WARD, Joshua
A quack doctor famed for his patent drop and pill. He tried to help the poor with free hospitals and he was patronized by the King.

WELSTED, Leonard
Clerk in the government. Pope quarrelled with him for 'explaining' some allusions in his poems, including that to Timon as Chandos.

WEST, John, Earl de la Warr
Among Walpole's most able and watchful supporters.

YONGE, Sir William
A Whig politician and sometime Secretary for War; a good-humoured, harmless man with a proverbial reputation for being at war.